Praise for *I Am the Central Park Jogger*

"The best hero stories are never about facing and vanquishing an enemy, though that might be the narrative. The real showdown is with one's self. . . . Trisha Meili had to figure out why life was worth the pain of forging ahead when giving in offered painless escape. . . . Maybe until you're in such a predicament, you can't mine your soul for its hidden steel."

—*San Francisco Chronicle*

"Its moments of unexpected grace and insights into life's challenges are hugely rewarding. Meili's story—the story the public never knew—is unforgettable."

—*The Buffalo News*

"[Meili's] tale of her recovery is also a passionate and inspirational guide for those suffering from traumatic brain injuries and other seemingly insurmountable, debilitating conditions."

—*The Cleveland Plain Dealer*

"Forced to accept first her physical, then her intellectual limitations, she lets go of the old, preattack Trisha. She is reborn. It is a double healing. It is a modest celebration of inner peace, the attainment of which is a mighty achievement—and one well worth recording."

—*Daily Mail* (London)

"Riveting."

—*Orlando Sentinel*

"Inspiring others in their recovery appears to be [Meili's] role in what she calls her 'second life.' She has made a good start with this book."

—*Pittsburgh Post-Gazette*

"The book is inspirational and encompasses the power of the human spirit. Through it, Meili is seen not as a victim, but as a survivor."

—*San Antonio Express-News*

"Trisha Meili is a brave person . . . She has come forward with a book that captures in harrowing detail all she has suffered, and all she has still accomplished . . . it will certainly earn its author the admiration of every reader."

—*Fort Worth Star-Telegram*

I AM THE
CENTRAL PARK JOGGER

A Story of
Hope and Possibility

TRISHA MEILI

Scribner
NEW YORK LONDON TORONTO SYDNEY

SCRIBNER
1230 Avenue of the Americas
New York, NY 10020

First Scribner trade paperback edition 2004

SCRIBNER and design are trademarks of
Macmillan Library Reference USA, Inc., used under license
by Simon & Schuster, the publisher of this work.

For information about special discounts for bulk purchases,
please contact Simon & Schuster Special Sales:
1-800-456-6798 or business@simonandschuster.com

Designed by Kyoko Watanabe
Text set in Berling

Manufactured in the United States of America

7   9   10   8

Library of Congress Cataloging-in-Publication Data is available.

ISBN-13: 978-0-7432-4437-4
ISBN-10:   0-7432-4437-0
ISBN-13: 978-0-7432-4438-1 (Pbk)
ISBN-10:   0-7432-4438-9 (Pbk)

*To all those who have helped and
continue to help me heal*

Contents

Contents

How could we forget those ancient myths that stand at the beginning of all races, the myths about dragons that at the last moment are transformed into princesses? Perhaps all the dragons in our lives are princesses who are only waiting to see us act, just once, with beauty and courage. Perhaps everything that frightens us is, in its deepest essence, something helpless that wants our love.

RAINER MARIA RILKE: *Letters to a Young Poet*
Translated by Stephen Mitchell

I AM THE
CENTRAL PARK JOGGER

Prologue

"I've got news," Elizabeth Lederer, the chief prosecutor in my case, said over the phone. Her voice was controlled; I could tell she was trying to hide her emotion.

Her call came in early June 2002, when I was more than halfway through the writing of this book, and left me too stunned to respond. Matias Reyes, a convicted murderer and serial rapist serving thirty-three years to life, claimed he alone had dragged me into a ravine, raped me, and left me for dead. DNA evidence placed him at the crime scene. He could not be charged because the statute of limitations in the case had expired.

As the ensuing investigation wore on, I struggled to understand the implications. We had always known there was another involved in the attack, so that part of his confession merely told us his identity. But if he was telling the truth that he had acted alone, then the five who had been convicted for the crimes against me were innocent. Questions assailed me. Could Reyes be believed? What if the wrong people had gone to jail? To what degree would I again be involved if there was a new investigation?

What I thought was a closed chapter in my life was reopened. Headlines screamed "Jogger" once again. I was living the horror as I had not lived it before, since I had been beaten into a coma the first time around.

Reyes became real to me in a way the five had not. I didn't want to see him in the paper, hear him talk on the television news. He had murdered a woman and raped more, forcing some at knifepoint to make a choice: "Your eyes or your life." How the hell did I survive?

But through all the recent developments, one thing remained constant: there is nothing I can add or contribute to what happened that night. The traumatic brain injury inflicted on me leaves me unable to remember anything of the attack. In a way, that makes me feel helpless. Not as a victim, but as someone who wants to contribute to the truth. Part of my being at peace with the events of April 19, 1989, however, is accepting that I will never know.

On the morning of December 19, 2002, New York State justice Charles J. Tejada announced his decision to vacate the convictions of five young men—Antron McCray, Raymond Santana, Yusef Salaam, Kevin Richardson, and Kharey Wise—for various combinations of robbery, riot, assault, sexual abuse, rape, sodomy, and attempted murder in Central Park that April. New York's Criminal Procedure Law—Section 440.10 (1) (g)—provides that, among other criteria, if "new evidence" is such that it would probably have resulted in a verdict more favorable to the defendant if it had been received at trial, then a court may vacate the convictions. After the judge did just that—vacated the convictions—the Manhattan District Attorney said he would not seek a retrial.

But these developments have not changed my purpose in writing this book. It has taken me fourteen years to go public with my story, and that story isn't about the justice system, about who attacked me, or whether one confession or five were true. It is about reclaiming a life, *my* life.

I built a life until I was twenty-eight, was struck down, and so had to build another. Two lives, and I'm proud of both. My book is about something I did, not what was done to me. I needed help, and my story is also about the nature and effect of that help.

I offer my story and the lessons I learned as an invitation to heal.

Preface

"I'm Okay"

Shortly after 9 P.M. on April 19, 1989, a young woman, out for her run in New York's Central Park, was bludgeoned, raped, sodomized, and beaten so savagely that doctors despaired for her life and a horrified nation cried out in pain and outrage.

I am that woman, until now known only as the Central Park Jogger, and this is my story.

For fourteen years I've been reluctant to tell it, despite repeated entreaties from magazines, book publishers, and movie and television studios. I was counseled—and believed—that only by remaining anonymous could I return to the normality of my life before the attack. Well, I'm "normal" now; I'm okay. And many other factors have convinced me that it's time to write about my experiences under my real name. But I've not "returned" to the young, ambitious, workaholic associate of the Energy and Chemicals Group in the Corporate Finance Department of Salomon Brothers. My physical and cognitive abilities are different. Different things matter to me. What I value is different, though my values haven't changed. I see the world through different eyes and am more appreciative of the people, places, and life around me.

I went for a run and had my life interrupted. No one comes that close to death without being transformed in some way, and I've learned to accept the changes, both positive and negative. After April 19, the world reached out to me because I was so brutally attacked, and I benefited profoundly from the outpouring of support. Now I'm reaching back out to the world. I'm proud to tell you that my name is Trisha Meili. To be able to write this at all represents an important breakthrough in my healing.

◆

Mention the Central Park Jogger to virtually any adult in New York City, and to millions across the country, and they'll relive their sense of shock at what happened to her, even fourteen years later. I'm not sure why this is so. In the intervening years, there have unfortunately been innumerable beatings and countless rapes (during the week I was attacked, twenty-eight other rapes were reported across the city), yet my case is remembered while the others are forgotten by all but the victims, the victims' immediate families and friends. Perhaps it is because this assault revealed the basest depravity human beings are capable of—the attack was believed to have been committed by a group of teenagers between the ages of fourteen and sixteen, out only to have some "fun"—and people shuddered to realize such cruelty exists in our exalted species. Perhaps it is also the randomness of the attack (Tom Wicker, in a *New York Times* column, called the act "inexplicable"), the sense that "there but for the grace of God go I." And perhaps it is because people wanted to affirm that there is a better, higher part in the vast majority of us and could display that nobility in their desire to comfort me. That comfort, expressed through prayer, through letters, through gifts, through kindness, played an essential part in my recovery. The love and support I received from so many surely motivated me to keep pushing ahead and moving forward.

For more than ten years I've been looking for a way to turn what was truly horrible into something positive, to use my experience as the basis for inspiration, not pity. As it turned out, the attack, meant to take my life, gave me a deeper life, one richer and more meaningful than it might have been. A newspaper reporter once dubbed me "Lady Courage." I was proud of that description, a recognition that what I was going through wasn't easy; it took hard work to recover; and even today the process continues. It took courage to give up my privacy. I never intended to become famous or an inspiration. I am an ordinary woman who experienced an extraordinary trauma. But as the years passed, the ideas I wanted to express became clearer in my mind, continued to nag at me, and I felt compelled to take the risk of stepping out of my privacy. My story is not essentially about violence in the cities nor the success or failure of our criminal justice system. Nor is it about vengeance or hate.

Rather it is about the capacity of the human body and spirit to heal.

◆

It is also about power. Not military power or corporate power, but powers that are far more important and eternal. The power of touch, for example, and the power of intention. The power of the body and the power of the mind. The power of doing. The power of no resentment. All these were shown to me during my rehabilitation.

In May 2001, my mother died unexpectedly. She was an important figure in my life, perhaps *too* important. There is probably no greater pain to a mother than to see her child suffer, and while she was alive, she fought fiercely to keep our tragedy private. The attack on me was also an attack on her and on our entire family, for my suffering, as a therapist said, had a ripple effect that sent waves of hurt to all of them. Still, in my final conversation with my mom, she supported my desire to use my experience to help others. Her passing was in one way a release, a sign that I had her permission to write about what had happened to me and what I had learned from it.

Another motivation to write is a recent experience of speaking at a rehabilitation hospital. I was there at the invitation of Dr. Jon Kabat-Zinn, founder and former director of the Stress Reduction Clinic at the University of Massachusetts Medical Center. Our audience was a large group of clinicians and patients in various stages of recovery from head injuries. This was my first time "going public," and I was not sure of the response.

It was the confirmation of my audience more than my own

prepared words that calmed me down. Some of the people had severe head injuries and asked about my own. I told them that I had overheard the phrases "brain damaged" and "permanently injured" and "she'll only be able to come back so far," and I had fooled the speakers (usually doctors) by the extent of my recovery and they might too. I didn't make false promises, I only said what was true for me, yet it was obvious that I had struck a chord. One man in a wheelchair, who had been in a coma for fourteen weeks, was thrilled that I had been in a wheelchair too and was now walking—not perfectly, but walking. He told me I had given him great motivation, and that he would "beat this"— his own disability. His faith was as powerful to me as mine was to him. Another asked me how I had come so far on my own, and I said I hadn't done it on my own, that doctors, nurses, therapists, family, friends, and strangers had given me hope, and from hope there emerges possibility.

I saw that my answers inspired my listeners, and I realized that I would have to write my story down in the belief that I might reach others. This book is the result.

Chapter One

"Wilding"

At 5 P.M. on the day of the assault, I turned down a dinner invitation from a friend because I had too much work to do at the office. This was not unusual. At age twenty-eight, I was on the fast track at Salomon Brothers, one of the top-tier investment banks on Wall Street, and often worked late; it was one way to stay on the track.

Before I left the office, Pat Garrett, a colleague of mine who worked in the adjoining cubicle, asked my advice about a new stereo. Three months earlier I had moved into a building on East 83rd Street and had bought a system that I had described to Pat as ideal for a smallish New York apartment.

"Why not come over and take a look at it?" I suggested.

"Sure," he said, delighted. We had become good friends at Salomon, though our romantic attachments lay elsewhere.

"Come around ten. That'll give me time to go for a run before you get there."

There was no chance I'd forgo the run. I was obsessed with exercise and had run marathons in Boston and many 10K races in New York City. Since I normally arrived at work at seven-thirty, running in the morning would have meant getting up too early. Besides, a night jog was a fine way to relieve the stress of the day. I varied my route occasionally, as the mood struck me, but often, after entering Central Park on 84th Street, would turn north to the 102nd Street crossdrive. At night, this area of the park was secluded and dimly lit, but the only concession I made to its potential danger was to go there at the beginning of my run, rather than later at night. That friends had warned me about running alone at all at night may have goaded me to continue. I had been running there for two and a half years without their advice, and I didn't need it now. Like many young people, I felt invincible. Nothing would happen to me. I can be determined, defiant, headstrong—and maybe there were deeper issues that drove me to take the risk.

"Great," Pat said. "I'll be there at ten."

And while I remember the five-o'clock call, I don't remember the conversation with Pat; I've reconstructed it here after later talks with him. Indeed, the dinner invitation is my last memory of anything—words, events, people, actions, touch, sights, pain, pleasure, emotions; *anything*—until nearly six weeks later.

◆

Just before nine that night, a group of more than thirty teenagers gather on 110th Street, the northern end of Central Park, for a night of "wilding"—senseless violence performed because it's "fun and something to do."* They throw rocks and bottles at cars entering the park; punch, kick, and knock down a Hispanic man, drag him nearly unconscious into the bushes, pour beer over him, and steal his food. They decide not to attack a couple walking along the path because the two are on a date, but do go after a couple on a tandem bicycle, who manage to elude them. They split into smaller groups, then come together, then split again, like dancers in a sinister ballet. In all, eight are assaulted, including a forty-year-old teacher and ex-marine named John Loughlin, whom they beat unconscious.

Reports from that time allege that between eight and fifteen of them spot a young woman jogging alone along the 102nd Street crossdrive. There they tackle her, punch her, and hit her with a sharp object. Soon they drag her down into a ravine where one of the teenagers rips off her jogging pants. The woman is in excellent condition, and she kicks and scratches at them, screaming wildly; it is difficult to pin down her arms and legs. Finally, she is hit in the left side of the face with a brick or rock. Her eye socket shatters and she stops fighting and screaming.

By this time, John Loughlin, having regained consciousness,

---

*Since I have no memory of the events, I've relied on accounts from myriad newspaper and magazine articles written at the time, as well as from *Unequal Verdicts: The Central Park Jogger Trials*, by Timothy Sullivan. These accounts were largely based on often conflicting statements given by some of the teenagers when first questioned by authorities as well as on statements by victims of other attacks that night. Matias Reyes's confession, however, has raised serious questions about the initial accounts given by the teens.

has been found by the police and reported his assault. He is taken to a hospital. The cops, now aware of the attacks from reports by some of the victims, have fanned out, looking for the assailants. The park goes quiet.

Three and a half hours later, two policemen, Robert Calaman and Joseph Walsh, sitting in an unmarked car at the 102nd Street crossdrive, are approached by two Latino men, shouting excitedly about a man in the woods who has been beaten and tied up. The policemen drive closer to investigate. Walsh gets out of the car and sees a body in the mud off the pavement, lying faceup and thrashing violently.

The men were wrong. It is the body of a woman. Naked except for her bra, which has been pushed above her breasts; her running shirt has been used to gag her and tie her hands in a praying position in front of her face. Walsh tells her he's a policeman.

"Who did this to you?" he asks. "Can you speak to me?"

There is no response. She is bleeding profusely. One of her eyes is puffed out, almost closed. The policemen call an ambulance. EMTs arrive. She is taken to Metropolitan Hospital, known for its acute-trauma care, and rushed to the emergency room. She is met by Dr. Isaac Sapozhnikov, attending physician in the ER, who instantly calls Dr. Robert S. Kurtz, director of Surgical Intensive Care, at his home. Dr. Kurtz issues instructions for the immediate care the Jogger needs and comes in early that morning. He will supervise her treatment for the seven weeks she is at Metropolitan.

It is astonishing that the Jogger is alive. She is in deep shock, her blood pressure so low that the ER staff are unable to get an accurate reading. Her body temperature is eighty-five degrees, and she is unable to breathe on her own. A technician stands by her side to pump oxygen down a tube in her throat. Last rites are administered.

The woman is bleeding from five deep cuts across her forehead and scalp; patients who lose this much blood are generally dead. Her skull has been fractured, and her eye will later have to be put back in its place. When it comes time for surgery, Kurtz will be surrounded by a crackerjack team: two plastic surgeons, an expert on severe injuries to the eye; an ear, nose, and throat specialist. But for now, he—and Dr. Sapozhnikov before him— has only the emergency room staff to assist him.

The victim's arms and legs are flailing violently, the aftereffects of massive brain damage, and that night have had to be tied to the gurney since there are not enough night nurses to monitor her constantly. The jerking and thrashing mean that both halves of her brain have lost their ability to control the movement of her extremities, to say nothing of her ability to think or feel. Many will stand by her bed in coming days and interpret this as the Jogger still fighting for her life.

There is extreme swelling of the brain caused by the blows to the head. The probable result is intellectual, physical, and emotional incapacity, if not death. Permanent brain damage seems inevitable.

◆

As promised, Pat gets to Trisha's apartment building at ten. He rings up. No answer. Funny, he thinks, she must still be in the shower. He waits, rings again. When there's no response, he goes to a phone booth at the corner and calls her. He gets her machine. "Hi, I'm not able to answer the phone right now, but if you'll leave your name and number . . ."

"Trisha, where are you? It's the story of my life, women always standing me up," he jokes. "I'm going home. Hope everything's okay." A tendril of worry takes root, grows. How could she have forgotten that they were supposed to meet? He calls Trisha's former boyfriend, Paul Raphael, since Paul and Trisha often ran together. Paul doesn't know where she is either. Pat considers calling the police, but doesn't, thinking they'd laugh at him. It's a regret he carries to this day.

Trisha is usually the first one in the office, so when Pat gets in around eight the next morning and doesn't see her, the alarm bell rings more loudly in his brain. He asks Joanne, Trisha's secretary, if she might be traveling. No, Joanne answers. His concern mounts.

Meanwhile, Peter Vermylen, a more senior member of Salomon's Energy and Chemicals Group, and one of the people who has strongly warned Trisha against running in the park at night, is driving from his home in New Jersey to the PATH train that will take him to New York City. On the way, he listens to a radio report so disturbing that when he gets to the parking lot, he stays in his car until it finishes. A young woman has been attacked in Central Park, and he knows that Trisha jogs there almost every night.

He reaches Salomon Brothers and looks toward Trisha's desk. It is empty. She usually gets in before he does, he thinks. He asks Joanne if she has heard from Trisha. She says no. He asks her to call Trisha's apartment. No answer. Deeply worried now, he decides to contact the police, and after a couple of unproductive calls he reaches the precinct where a group of detectives have been assigned to the case. He tells the detective who answers the phone that he might know the victim and gives him Trisha's name, age, occupation. The detective describes the victim's hair as curly and medium brown, and Peter feels reassured: Trisha's is dirty blond and straight. But then the detective asks if the woman wears a "distinctive piece of jewelry." Peter puts his hand over the mouthpiece and asks Joanne about it. She describes it to him—it is a gold ring shaped into a bow—and he passes the information to the detective. "It's her," the detective says, and Peter hears him call to his colleagues, "We've got her. She's an investment banker." He asks Peter additional questions, but Peter can't talk. He's gasping for breath.

He calls Terry Connelly in Administration with the news. The detectives want someone from the firm to go to the hospital to identify the victim, and Peter volunteers for the job. No, Terry says, he'll go himself, along with a close friend of Trisha's, Pat Garrett. Peter tells him about the ring.

Pat and Terry go together to Metropolitan Hospital. They're stopped by a security guard in the lobby. The place is a madhouse. Cops are everywhere. Reporters clamor for access and information.

"No one's allowed up," the guard tells them.

"But I'm here to identify her," Pat insists.

"We'll show you a picture."

It's impossible to identify the woman in the picture; her face is unrecognizable. Pat insists on seeing Trisha in person. His reason tells him the woman in the photograph with her battered body, swollen face, and puffy eyes is Trisha. But emotionally, he's not prepared to say, "Yeah, that's her."

Reluctantly, a policeman escorts the two men upstairs. There is a guard outside Trisha's door, and a small group of doctors and nurses whispering nearby. Otherwise, silence. Pat opens the door, looks down at the figure on the bed. The woman's head is covered by bandages. Her face is so badly beaten and swollen it looks like some grotesque Halloween mask, barely human. Pat can't believe that the body before him is alive. He's still not positive it is his dear friend who is lying in front of him. A policeman enters, shows him the ring the victim wore—and Pat's heart breaks. It is a little golden bow.

Pat calls the office to ask Joanne for numbers from Trisha's Rolodex and embarks on one of the most difficult jobs he's ever had to do: he must break the news to Trisha's family.

The cops have been busy. Acting on tips and interviews, they have soon winnowed out suspects from the group allegedly in the park, among them Steve Lopez, fifteen; Antron McCray, fifteen; Raymond Santana, fourteen; Yusef Salaam, fifteen; Kevin Richardson, fourteen; and Kharey Wise, sixteen. They are black and Hispanic. Some live in Schomburg Plaza, a government-subsidized housing development directly north of Central Park, others in the Taft Houses project on Madison Avenue. Most are from two-parent, blue-collar environments. Nothing in their outward circumstances would mark them as capable of this violence. When two are put into Rikers Island prison, they are beaten by other inmates furious at the nature of their alleged crime.

On April 20, Elizabeth Lederer, one of New York's top prosecutors and a renowned trial attorney, is assigned to the Jogger case by Linda Fairstein, head of the Sex Crimes Prosecution Unit; it has been put in Fairstein's department because technically this is a sex crime, not yet a homicide. Lederer, already alerted that she will be the lead prosecutor in the case, goes to the 20th Precinct on West 82nd Street at 8 P.M. The investigation has been moved here from the much smaller Central Park station house, where some of the teens were initially taken and interrogated by detectives for hours. Primed by the police, Lederer spends the rest of the night of the twentieth and day of the twenty-first getting on videotape most of the suspects' individual responses to her questions about the attack. The parents of some are there for the questioning, as is usually required for suspects under the age of sixteen, since otherwise what they say may not be admissible as evidence in a trial.

Some of the teenagers are arrogant and hostile; some are more subdued. Some admit to being part of the group who assailed the jogger; one—Wise—tells Lederer "this is my first rape." Later, confessions will be recanted and the defense will argue that they were coerced. Though divergent in many respects, and though no clear physical evidence links the teens to the crime, the stories have enough similarities in their details to convince Lederer they are true. At the same time they point blame in so many different directions that she knows the task of putting together a solid, irrefutable scenario of the events of April 19 to present to a jury will be Herculean.

◆

The media goes into a frenzy. New York City in 1989, as *New York Times* columnist Bob Herbert later describes it, is "a city soaked in the blood of crime victims. Rapists, muggers, and other violent criminals seemed to roam the city at will. . . . Someone was murdered every four or five hours." The "Jogger case" speaks to the city's worst fears, its deepest divisions, and indeed the nation's fears and divisions. The major national stories that have occupied the press—the spread of the spill of oil from the *Exxon Valdes*, the closing arguments in the Iran/contra trial, the scandal involving House Speaker Jim Wright—are pushed to the sidelines. Because the body wasn't discovered until the early-morning hours of the twentieth, full morning newspaper coverage doesn't begin until the twenty-first, though the afternoon papers already had the story. Once it starts, it doesn't stop. It is the lead story on local and national television for many days, and the newspaper coverage is even more extensive. Beyond the papers in the immediate area, the story is picked up within days by the *Boston Globe, San Francisco Chronicle, Los Angeles Times, Northern Virginia Daily, USA Today, Seattle Times, Detroit News, Pittsburgh Post Gazette, Houston Chronicle, Dallas Times Herald,* and *Milwaukee Journal,* among others. The *International Herald Tribune* runs a long story on the Jogger, and the case is covered both in the *Evening Standard* of London and *La Presse Étrangère* in Lebanon. A special hospital spokesperson is assigned to brief the media first hourly, then daily. As soon as they can, weekly and monthly magazines feature the Jogger and/or her alleged assailants. All three major women's magazines—*Ladies' Home Journal, Good Housekeeping,* and *McCall's*—have comprehensive coverage. In December, the Jogger is chosen as one of *Glamour's* Women of the Year, and *People* magazine names her one of the Year's Most Interesting People.

There is an unwritten law among journalists that names of

rape victims are not to be revealed, and in this case only a few break the rule, notably the *Amsterdam News*, New York City's leading African-American paper, which urges fairness for the teenagers. Sensationalist headlines are everywhere. The teens are described as a "Wolf Pack"; there is a strident call to bring back the death penalty. The fate of the victim has resonances that affect the hearts of the journalists themselves, and although many of them know her identity, their obvious empathy and sympathy keep them quiet.

◆

Family and friends begin to arrive at the hospital, among them several Salomon employees including Kevin O'Reilly, the Jogger's boyfriend at the time, though few at Salomon know this. When the Jogger's aunt, Barbara Murphy, gets there from New Jersey, she is amazed to see "men in suits" clustered outside the victim's room. Then one of the Jogger's two brothers, Steve, thirty-two, a labor lawyer, hurries in. He lives in Hartford, Connecticut, and was the first person Pat Garrett called from Metropolitan after identifying the victim. The Jogger's parents, Jack, a retired marketing manager at Westinghouse, and Jean, a homemaker, Republican committeewoman, and eight-year school director on the Upper St. Clair School Board, fly in from their home near Pittsburgh. Salomon sends a limousine to pick them up, but, not expecting one, they miss connections and take a cab to the hospital. The cab door is opened by a policeman who has been alerted to expect them, and he escorts them into the hospital.

The Jogger's other brother, Bill, thirty-five, an assistant district attorney in Dallas, arrives from Texas. By the time he gets to his sister's room, someone has cleared the surroundings of all but doctors, nurses, and family members. (Steve will later stand guard against reporters trying to worm their way into the waiting room or overhear conversations in the corridor; one even disguises himself as an orderly and tries to get into the Jogger's room that way.) Now the Jogger's closest relatives have each had a chance to look at her. Gathered in the visitors' waiting room, they grasp the extent of the tragedy. The sporadic movements of the Jogger's arms and legs are her only signs of life. Her face is unrecognizable, even to them. That night, one family member asks the doctors to remove the restraints, but is told it's too dangerous. She might hurt herself or pull out one of the many tubes—for breathing, for food, for elimination, for the monitoring of heart and other functions. Salomon will pay for full-time private nurses to attend her.

The family members meet in a conference room, where they are visited by Dr. Kurtz. He is not reassuring. They will set up a round-the-clock vigil at her bedside, in eight-hour shifts, until—they dare not finish the sentence. Day after day passes, and their beloved Trisha is still comatose.

◆

New York City itself goes into mourning. The rape of a slim, seemingly frail, innocent woman—she weighs less than one hundred pounds—seems a rape of the city itself, and her fate becomes the major topic of discussion in every borough, every community. Some call her foolish for venturing into the park at night, but *New York Times* columnist Tom Wicker affirms in her "the primacy of freedom over fear—all honor to her for that."

Mayor Ed Koch, who has offered Trisha's parents lodging at Gracie Mansion (they refuse), calls for a day of prayer, and churches, synagogues, and mosques hold special services. Many in the black community are defensive, warning that those in custody might be unjustly accused. Others are sympathetic. Neighbors of the suspects hold a prayer vigil outside the hospital. Members of four of the suspects' families send flowers and express their grief.

Metropolitan Hospital is besieged by strangers wishing to help in any way they can, and a separate location is set up where blood can be donated to replenish that given to the Jogger. Salomon sets up a blood-donation center for its employees as well. The hospital switchboard is overwhelmed by calls asking for information about the Jogger's condition or simply conveying good wishes and prayers for her recovery. Flowers pour in from all over the country, including eighteen roses from Frank Sinatra. None beyond the immediate family know that a doctor, though not Dr. Kurtz, has told them in a moment of particular brutality that "it might be better for all if Trisha died."

◆

The attack hits the people at Salomon Brothers particularly hard. John H. Gutfreund, chairman and chief executive officer, and Tom Strauss, president, were told immediately of the tragedy, and an attempt was made to keep the news from the employees until there could be more definitive word on the Jogger's fate. This was futile, and on the first day the company is in shock. Gutfreund and Strauss go to the hospital, and soon many other Salomon employees are traveling to Metropolitan to pay their respects. Trisha has made a special effort to be friendly with her coworkers—reserve has long been a character trait and she has battled against it—and has succeeded. She is in fact loved, which adds heightened emotion to the suspense. Will she survive? her colleagues wonder. Will she ever wake from her coma?

On the twenty-first, a notice from Gutfreund goes to all employees:

> There will be a service of prayer for the recovery of
> Trisha Ellen Meili at the Church of the Heavenly Rest,
> Fifth Avenue and 90th Street, tomorrow, Saturday,
> April 22, at 6:00 P.M.
> Please bring a candle.

Lisa Borowitz from the Corporate Communications Department is assigned to handle all calls coming into the firm regarding Trisha—for a while there are some two hundred a day. She will remain in that job for many months. And the company does much more. The Meili family has a comfortable income, but the medical bills, beyond Trisha's insurance coverage, will be staggering. For starters, in addition to the cost of the private nurses, Salomon will also pay her hospital costs.

◆

At first, the Jogger's survival is the key issue. There is a terrible moment on April 27 when the breathing tube is removed and it is found the Jogger can't breathe on her own—it's the only time, Dr. Kurtz testifies at the trials of the defendants, that he felt like crying.

A second extubation is done on May 2; the crisis is resolved. Still, questions about her eventual recovery haunt everyone. It is soon probable that the patient will survive, but in what condition? The worry revolves around the long-term damage to the brain. Will she be able to walk—let alone run—again? Once the eye is repaired and the socket rebuilt, how will her vision be affected? What about her fine-motor skills? Will she be able to fend for herself without assistance? Will she ever be able to live alone? What about her capacity for speech, for memory, for reasoning? No one knows or dares predict the outcome.

◆

Some of the care is nonmedical. Along with Trisha's family, Pat Babb, one of the private nurses, is especially loving and attentive. After some five days, there is physical therapy, even if it is only stretching the patient's arms and legs and exercising her ears and nose by pulling on them while she remains in a deep coma. Even before Trisha can talk, a psychiatrist, Mary Ann Cohen, begins neurological rehabilitation. She stands by the bed, telling Trisha where she is and that she is surrounded by those who care for her. Each family member speaks gently to her, assuring her of his or her love. There are few signs that the comatose woman internalizes any of this, but the psychiatrist and the Meili family are convinced it helps.

◆

The Jogger's pulse quickens when her mother speaks to her and holds her hand—but she remains comatose for twelve days, and when she is at last semiconscious, she can identify a few words and objects, as Dr. Kurtz reports to the press and to Gutfreund at Salomon.

On May 3, fourteen days after the attack, Gutfreund sends another memo to the Salomon employees:

> We thought you might be pleased to read the latest
> report (3 P.M. today) issued by Trisha Meili's doctor at
> Metropolitan Hospital: "Today we are happy to state that
> favorable trends that began to manifest yesterday
> culminated in removal of the patient from the ventilator.
> She can now utter single- and two-word phrases. She can
> also read signs with her name on them, as well as the
> words Yes and No. When told that a nurse at her bedside
> wanted to take up jogging, the patient replied 'me too.'
> While her neurological condition is still far from normal,
> patient is now out of a coma. She still has a low-grade
> temperature but overall has improved markedly over the
> last two days."

The report does not go into great detail. Coming "out of a coma," which actually began on May 1, is a gradual process. It does not mean the Jogger has regained her memory or sense of self, nor that she realizes what has happened to her or where she is. She can identify simple words on flash cards, gasp a hoarse hello to her father, move her eyebrows voluntarily. "She still suffers moments of delusion and fluctuates between lucid and unresponsive," Dr. Kurtz tells the *New York Times*. She is still in critical condition. And her parents have had to sneak out of their hotel through its kitchen to avoid the press stationed in the lobby and anxious for their reaction to the signs of progress. They know something the media does not: their daughter has pneumonia.

On May 8, there is another memo from Gutfreund:

> The following is an update on the medical condition of Trisha Meili, as reported by Dr. Robert S. Kurtz, Director of the Surgical Intensive Care Unit at Metropolitan Hospital Center. Dr. Kurtz said: "Our patient's maximum temperature in the last 24 hours was 100.4, but at present she does not have a fever. Over the weekend the patient had a transient period of reduced alertness. However, a repeated CAT scan of her head disclosed no new pathology and the patient has returned to her previous state of alertness. She is still not well oriented to time and place, though she has now for the first time made reference to some of her friends and family members. Today she was able, for the first time as well, to help in transferring herself from stretcher to bed. Her pneumonia of last week continues to resolve but we're maintaining a close watch for any further sign of infection. However, a gallium scan designed to search for sources of infection thus far has shown nothing new. We still consider her to be in critical condition."

And on May 9, another memo, also quoting Dr. Kurtz:

> "Our patient's maximum temperature was 99.7 which implies continued healing of her pneumonia. The patient shows further evidence of slow progress in recovery from

neurological injuries. She is able to name objects today such as a stethoscope which she was only able to describe by function but not name last week. Her orientation to time and place has improved but is still not complete.

"We plan to repair the patient's facial features including the bony supporting structure of the eye. The date tentatively set is May 17th, assuming no change in the patient's condition occurs.

"We would now classify the patient as being in serious rather than critical condition."

The bulletins hearten all who read them. What they do not reflect, however, are the dangers the Jogger faces.

◆

After an examination undertaken two weeks after the coma eases, her neuropsychologist issues a highly pessimistic report. It reads in part:

Summary and Recommendations: The patient is a 28 year old woman who sustained a severe head injury with excessive blood loss, resulting in moderately severe cerebral edema and coma lasting about two weeks. Approximately two weeks post-coma, she presents with signs of severe cognitive dysfunction suggestive of widespread cerebral impairment which is in the process of recovery. At this point, she manifests limitations in all areas of cognitive functioning. Even so, there have been some signs of incremental gains in specific areas over the course of several days. Most limiting at present are problems with attention and concentration, perseveration, memory and construction skills.

The severity of the patient's condition raises serious concerns about her prospects for long-term recovery. <u>However, it is far too early to make predictions concerning outcome.</u> . . .

Once the patient's acute medical needs are met, the present findings strongly suggest that she will require an intensive rehabilitation program that specializes in the treatment of patients with traumatic brain injury. . . . Several months after placement in a . . . rehabilitation program, it is suggested an independent neuropsychological assessment be undertaken to evaluate her progress and assist in long-term planning.

This evaluation is not included in bulletins to the press.

◆

And so it went, doctors working nonstop to save my life, neurologists watching for signs of understanding, my family by my side, my friends visiting as often as they were allowed: continuous activity, continuous motion, continuous crisis—so much so that many on the staff were worried I was being overstimulated—and I aware of none of it. What I now know of these first weeks I learned from what I've read and been told.

Memory is a tricky facility. When asked to recall their earliest memories, children often remember things their parents told them rather than retrieving the event itself. In my case, entering a kind of second childhood at age twenty-eight, this was not much different.

I didn't just come out of the coma, all facilities on "go"; the recovery of even a small part of what were the capabilities of my brain and body was slow and incremental. And on the day the coma began to lift, I was running a temperature of 106. As my recovery progressed, I began to remember faces, words, pictures, the names of things. Sometimes the memory would last, sometimes disappear. (One of the common neurological tests is to ask the patient to identify an object, tell her what it is if she can't, and then ask for the same identification fifteen minutes later.) My family and my neurologists told me how my memory improved day after day. But as I write this, I have no memory at all of those first weeks at Metropolitan. My amnesia is as complete for that time as it is for the attack itself.

Indeed, my first memory is of an incident that took place on May 26, five and a half weeks after I was admitted. I was lying in bed. An old boyfriend of mine named Ken Hansen, who had evidently visited me many times before, was standing by the base of the bed next to my nurse. I had asked the nurse a question, but Ken answered it for her. (He later told me I had asked the same question many times and had evidently not registered the response.) I was furious. He always talked a lot, and here he was doing it again. How *dare* he answer a question not addressed to him? He went on talking, and this I remember vividly:

"Shut up, Ken," I said. "I want to hear it from *her.*"

Nothing like a gracious reentry into human society.

Chapter Two

Who Was I?

I have no memory of the attack and the five and a half weeks after, and that's a blessing, for I don't carry with me the horror and the humiliation of the event, much as I yearn to contribute to finding the truth about what happened that night. But I remember my preattack life well. For the most part, I look back on it with pleasure and not a little bewilderment.

Loving, generous parents; two supportive brothers; close friends; a fine academic career sparked by a competitive nature; a steady progress from high school to college to graduate school to Wall Street, exemplifying focus and commitment to achievement; a developing social consciousness; the capacity to love and be loved; a self-image of kindness, sensitivity, competence, and ambition. All of these, I believe, components of the deepest part of me, allowed me to survive the attack and kept my mind concentrating on my recovery rather than indulging in self-pity or becoming obsessed with destructive rage.

Yet some of the same values that fueled my success had a dark side. I harbored an unhealthy secret. I suffered from anorexia from age fifteen until the end of my time at graduate school, and, with less force, even through my early professional career. It signaled that something was badly amiss, but at that time, I paid little attention. I knew I had it, that it affected my relationships, and that it had some deep connection with my compulsive need to run, but I chose to downplay it.

My six-week plunge into darkness—being raped, beaten, left for dead, and lying comatose in a hospital—changed who I was. As fire turns sand to glass, so the attack forged a new me. The basic elements remained the same, but in a different form.

◆

I grew up in Paramus, New Jersey, in the 1960s. My neighborhood was filled with boys. There were a few girls too, and I did have a close girlfriend, Paula. But since my brother Steve was the dominant figure in my preteen social life, I associate my childhood with boys. Thanks to him, I was included in their games. I enjoyed the back-and-forth, the exploration of the life of a suburban child.

Those games, varying with the seasons, left their mark. Steve loved basketball and baseball and football, and thus I loved them too and became good enough at them so that I wasn't an embarrassment either to him or myself. The games Steve organized were for kids of all ages. I was forced to compete with older kids, older boys, and that streak in me remained strong throughout my life.

I had another brother, Bill. Since he was seven years older, he was a remote figure in my childhood, a kind of idol I worshiped but who paid little attention to me. "Were you fifteen when you were born? I just don't remember you before that," he kidded me, deigning to notice his young sister on one of his visits from law school. We did have some interaction when I was a kid—I remember trying to jump on him when I was mad at him, and he'd just put his arm out and hold me back, my fists flailing at air. It made me even madder.

Steve and Bill notwithstanding, my mother was far and away the key figure in all areas of my life. My father worked for Westinghouse as a sales manager and, as was common in those days, left the rearing of the children to his wife. Perhaps I was my father's favorite—you know, the only girl. Mom poured the most energy into us, trying to make sure that we would turn out well. A brilliant woman, she was trained in psychology, but abandoned her graduate studies at Wellesley (in those years, they offered postgraduate degrees) to marry my father. I never heard her second-guess her decision, but some of her ambition may have been transplanted to me. I would go places she had not been able to explore.

Transplanted ambition can be a mixed blessing, but as a child all I believed was that whatever she did was right, and I was obedient and nonconfrontational. She wanted me to be a model little girl, and I passively complied. When I was six, she entered me in a ballet class so I would learn "poise and grace," and I remember sometimes racing from the football field to change into tights for my dance class. This led to a strange collection of heroes: New York Met Tommy Agee, Pittsburgh Steeler Terry Bradshaw, and New York City Ballet dancers Edward Villella and Patricia McBride. When I was twelve, and the junior high school allowed female students to wear pants, my mother nevertheless insisted on dresses. Her feeling was that good grooming was a way of showing respect to the teacher. A year later, after we had moved to Pittsburgh—I was thirteen—she let me wear pants to school because everyone else did, but no jeans, *never* jeans. That line would not be crossed!

She was strict, but I knew she was my ally. We lived close to my elementary school, and I always walked home for lunch. Mom would be there waiting with a wholesome, carefully prepared meal. At the end of the school day I'd walk home with my friend Kathy and, with some envy, watch her unlock her front door and enter her empty house. She carried her own key. "How grown-up," I thought. "I'd like to be independent like her." But I distinctly remember my gratitude that Mom was home when I came through my own front door.

◆

Mom was a good cook, and when I was a young girl, dinners together in the dining room brought the five of us close together, a wonderful nightly ritual where we would discuss what we kids had done during the day.

Another place we came together was at church. Mom was Catholic, Dad Protestant. We were raised Catholic (Dad converted when I was in high school), and when I was a child, all of us went to mass on Sundays. I must confess that I often hoped the priest would use the shortest form of the mass, but I did enjoy being with my family.

My connection to religion changed when I left home and went to college. I stopped going to church. I questioned the idea of a higher power and felt insincere in professing a faith that believed in one. The image I had been led to believe, that of an old man with a beard who held sway over our lives, no longer felt comfortable. It was a matter of control. Giving myself up to an authority I couldn't connect to didn't fit with the practical, "show me the facts and numbers" side of me that emerged early in my adolescence and blossomed during my career.

The secular teachings of Catholicism were another matter. I think I was always conscious of trying to be a "good" person, and from an early age I've felt an obligation to treat other people well and to support and encourage them.

Studying hard brought rewards of a more immediate kind: praise, advancement, measurable success. It was something I thought I was expected to do, and I took the responsibility seriously, but I also enjoyed it, and not only because of the rewards. Both my parents were dedicated to education and continuously stressed its benefits to me and my brothers. Too, my own competitive nature drove me to excel. "Oh, my parents did well at school? I'll do well too." "My brothers got good grades? I'll get better ones." That was my attitude, and it served me well. Every year there was a new challenge, a new goal, a new competition.

All the work left me little time for dating, and when we

moved from Paramus to Pittsburgh, I avoided social pressure; I wasn't a party girl or member of the "in" crowd. I had crushes, of course, but they were on older, unattainable boys—juniors when I was a freshman, seniors when I was a sophomore. No matter. My focus on schoolwork left me one A away from valedictorian.

Like most girls, I loved horses and pleaded for riding lessons. Never mind that I was taking ballet classes a few days a week, or that I had a full academic schedule with extracurricular activities—yearbook editor, member of the student council—or that my parents were paying for college for Steve and Bill so the added expense would be a burden. I *had* to take up riding.

In my sophomore year, my parents finally agreed to lessons, and on Saturday mornings my father drove me to riding school, over an hour away. The classes were at 8 A.M., which meant the poor man had to get up at six, and often, in winter, it was freezing cold. The ring was indoors but unheated, so Dad would stay in the car to keep warm. He never complained. Though I felt bad about getting him out of bed early on the weekend, I reveled in our time together driving both to and from. I remember those drives for the particular closeness between us.

Spring meant the annual student riding show. My mother, who was deathly afraid of horses, probably because her sister had once gotten a concussion from a bad fall, was there with my dad, along with other parents. Until that time, we rode separately, one student at a time, but today we would all be together in the ring, the instructor in the center leading us.

I was proud of what I had accomplished in seven months,

even if I was the oldest in the beginners' class. "Walk," the instructor said, and with a prod of our knees the horses obeyed. "Canter" came the command, and we spurred our steeds onward. Then, disaster. The horse behind me ran up on my horse, and mine spooked and took a sudden ninety-degree turn into the ring. I wasn't holding on tightly enough with my legs and the centrifugal force threw me into the air.

Such was my mother's power over me that just before I hit the ground, I thought, "Oh, God, this can't happen. Mom's going to be even more afraid and she's going to kill me." Then rider and ground met with terrific force, and I felt a shock in my shoulder and excruciating pain. I had broken my arm at the shoulder and was lucky to have escaped worse damage.

The result was the onset of anorexia.

◆

To be a ballet dancer you have to be thin. Although already naturally skinny, my ostensible motive for not eating—the conscious reason—was that because I had broken my arm, I couldn't exercise, and by not exercising I would grow fat and, though still able to dance, I'd—horrors!—no longer have the "ideal" body type. When, eight weeks later, the cast came off and I was free to exercise again and dance again, I continued not eating, and now there was no conscious reason; I didn't bother looking for one.

The dining room, once a place of refuge, became a torture chamber because of my anorexia. "How am I going to make it look like I'm eating when I'm really not?" I asked myself, sitting tensely with raised fork or spoon pushing food around on my plate. "Why does everything have to revolve around these god-damned meals?" Not eating did not seem to me a punishment. It was having to *pretend* that was so difficult to bear.

After the attack, posttrauma psychotherapy made me see that my anorexia was in part a battle for independence from my mother, in part another manifestation of my competitiveness. I recognized how much influence she had over me. The anorexia was a struggle for my autonomy. This was something that was all mine. I wasn't the best student in my class—Brian Phillips was— nor was I the prettiest or most popular. But, by God, I could be the *thinnest*, and I set out on that path with the same fierceness I approached sports and academics.

I'm not hurting anyone, I told myself, not even me, for I feel fine. I don't drink, don't do drugs. And—glorious feeling!—it's my secret. I and I alone had complete control of it. (Of course, it was actually controlling me.) Nobody knew what I knew; I could hoard that knowledge, revel in it. And if anyone, especially my mom or my dad, suggested I should be eating more, that triggered an escalation. Less food, more secrecy.

"You're not eating, darling."

"Actually, I had a big lunch. I'm just not hungry."

It amazes me that I, an intelligent young woman, believed that nothing bad would happen to me because I was starving myself. There were adverse symptoms—irregular menstruation, for starters—that pointed to the contrary. Yet that's what I thought. Part of me *wanted* to be different, even at the cost of reason. I would take the frequent comment "Trisha, you're so thin" as a compliment. When Karen Carpenter, one of the singing group The Carpenters, died of anorexia, I avoided all the news reports on the case, and there were many. I remember reading about a disorder called bulimia and thinking, "Oh, that's terrible. Think what damage you could do to your esophagus by continuously throwing up. I wouldn't do that to my body. I'll just not eat! No damage then!"

My parents were deeply concerned. My mother was convinced that my amenorrhea was a result of hitting my head when, just like her sister, I'd fallen from the horse. At one point during my senior year in high school, they took me to the hospital for a series of tests, and all came out negative: I was in "perfect" health.

A doctor there supplied the answer: my at best irregular periods, my abnormal thinness, my disinterest in food—all stress-related. I was driving myself too hard at school; he prescribed rest and some fun.

I heard it all and agreed, knowing the real reason—the secret reason—and thinking, "I'm fooling the physician and I'm fooling my parents as well!" That was part of the pleasure. It never occurred to me that I was fooling myself.

◆

Since I was academically competitive, my plan in high school was to get good grades so I could get into a good college, just as in college I tried to get good summer jobs so I would have a head start in getting into a good graduate school and getting a good permanent job once I'd graduated.

For the college step, I chose Wellesley. Again, my competitive nature and my parents' expectations for my education led me to seek a prestigious school. Wellesley College was familiar because my mom had spent some graduate-school time there.

When I got to Wellesely, I thought I'd concentrate on economics, but took other courses to see if they might interest me more. No. I liked economics. Not loved it, understand; part of my personality was—is—that I'm readily adaptable. Majoring in economics made a lot of sense; it would no doubt be of use in my later career, whatever that was. So I began economics courses and continued them throughout college. I also studied psychobiology, a field then underinvestigated and underappreciated. It sparked the beginning of my interest in how the mind affects the body, and how the body affects the mind.

One economics professor at Wellesley had a huge influence on me, though I never took a course with him. Ken Hansen was "a guest in residence," the term for someone affiliated with the school who also lived as a "house mother" in a dorm—my dorm—making sure we undergraduates didn't get into trouble. In freshman year, I followed my high school pattern by applying myself to studies at the expense of a social life, though there were plenty of men around; Wellesley, a women's college, had an exchange program with MIT. I never went too far afield for dating, and sophomore year, I started to see Ken.

He was a friend first. Ken was attractive, shared many of my interests, and was close at hand. The result: we had to conduct our relationship in secret, for it was not good policy for a faculty member to be dating a student, even if she wasn't a student of his. How perfectly this suited me! Now I had two secrets, an eating disorder that did not seem disordered to me, and a "forbidden" love who was mine alone. The only person who knew of the affair was my good friend and hallmate Ardith Eicher, who faithfully guarded my secret.

We obviously couldn't be seen going to the movies or holding hands in a coffee shop, but we often ran together. Running had replaced ballet in my life. My passion started in the summer before I went to Wellesley when my brother Bill asked me if I wanted to join him for a run at the high school track. Even once around the quarter-mile track was tough, but I was overjoyed to be with Bill. There was a high in the feeling of accomplishment when I finished, and I was hooked.

Running was a wonderful release, a great stress-reducer. It got me into nature, and most importantly it kept my already too low weight down. In college, I ran virtually every afternoon, sometimes with friends, sometimes with Ken, sometimes alone, proud of myself for keeping so fit. So *thin*. Was this compulsiveness an addiction, running not for the love of the sport but out of psychological need? The easy answer is yes, because I went at it so hard and, no matter where I traveled, made sure it was part of my agenda; but it nevertheless gave me an enormous sense of independence and pleasure. It made me think that my eating disorder wasn't affecting me. Not only was I performing well academically, making Phi Beta Kappa my junior year, but I had the strength to run five to ten miles whenever I felt like it. Somehow my body compensated for the lack of food in an amazing way.

One spring, I stood among a crowd of screaming young women watching the Boston marathoners run through Wellesley, the exact halfway point of the race. I decided then that I would run it the next year, the marathon being the ultimate test for runners. Exciting as it was to see, I wanted to run, the adventure and challenge blotting out pain and fatigue.

A year later, I was an unregistered runner, a "back of the packer," nowhere near the truly strong runners, but that made no difference. There were the Wellesley women on either side of the running corridor, cheering us all on, and this time I ran past them, totally taken up by the rhythm of the race—a mile, two miles, thirteen miles, twenty-six miles, not at all exhausting, producing an exhilaration unlike any other I've known. Yes, I pushed myself obsessively in training; yes, there were psychological undercurrents motivating me. But I know on that day, I felt happy and free.

There was to be another marathon, one in New York, that would have far greater meaning.

◆

Ken had a strong interest in economic development in third world countries, and thanks to him and to a course on the subject, it became a passion of mine as well. Ken and I went to South Africa, seeing apartheid firsthand. I was incensed by the conditions, appalled at the number of unfulfilled lives symbolized by the White Only signs above building entrances. I saw wasted potential in the third world. Economic development, I believed, was where I might do some good, and I applied to various grad schools' international programs.

My economics professor wrote an embarrassingly fulsome letter of recommendation to grad school:

> Trisha possesses a strong commitment to social services and
> recently has shifted the focus of that commitment from
> domestic toward international concerns. Recent travels to
> Africa and Latin America have made her aware of the
> extent of economic and political injustices in the developing

world and she has responded with a desire to become
professionally involved in addressing these inequalities. Her
sense of commitment towards these issues reflects her
personal qualities of empathy and compassion.

I decided to pursue a joint program of business and international relations because I felt I'd be a stronger candidate for whatever opportunities lay ahead. Yale had programs in each. A business school wants you to have some work experience. Very well, I'd work. An *international* development organization, such as the World Bank (which at the time seemed an ideal place for my to-be talents), wants international experience. Very well, I'd get it. I was highly motivated, highly ambitious, and highly unsure of what my studies would lead to. It would become more clear, I thought, with more experience.

I worked for a small Boston consulting company for a year and was accepted at Yale for a joint business/international relations degree. During that first summer of graduate school, I got a job with the U.S. State Department in Zimbabwe as a junior foreign service officer. I worked in the Political/Economic section of the American embassy in Harare, and I helped allocate the Self-Help Development Project budget, analyzed and visited major developmental projects—schools, roads—and represented the embassy at government functions. It was fulfilling, eye-opening work, and it made the World Bank seem a good place to begin my career.

By that time, Ken and I had drifted apart—there was no real breakup, just a natural ending to our togetherness. We just realized that it wasn't right. I tend to stay in things longer than perhaps I should, and I think Ken shared the trait.

The next summer I got an internship at the World Bank, but it changed my mind about my future. It does vital work, but as opposed to the work in Zimbabwe, I had a desk job in a giant bureaucracy. Spreadsheets took the place of interaction with a fascinating culture. I chafed under the restrictions.

◆

Back at Yale for my last year, all the talk was of permanent jobs at investment banks or consulting companies. Those were the firms recruiting heavily on campus, those were the most sought-after industries. Nineteen-eighties America was not an introspective place but a material one. My own idealism was put on hold—there would be time to help change the world. My competitive nature took over. I wanted to pit myself against "the best and the brightest," and I thought, "Why don't I just *try* investment banking? Learn what it's all about. I'm not necessarily going to do it forever, but I want to see if I can measure up."

Representatives from Salomon Brothers came to Yale and after several interviews in both New Haven and New York made me an offer. I took the job, thinking I'd try it for a little while, and after that, who knows? I got an offer from Merrill Lynch too, but the fact that Salomon seemed to like my Zimbabwe experience—hardly your typical investment banking background—convinced me to choose them.

Even in graduate school, the conflict between my desire for independence and my need for nurturing continued. I *felt* independent, studied and dated and took weekend trips, made friends. But the anorexia persisted. While I was physically away from my mother, I was still psychologically tied to her. When I dutifully went home for the holidays, mealtimes remained painful and I dreaded them. Yet still I ignored or at least downplayed the symptom. I was "fine."

Anorexia was a distancing mechanism, affecting dating and inhibiting the normal socializing with friends around meals. Only once did I have an open, honest discussion of the disorder with a man I went out with. He said, "You know, this is a real problem. You need to do something about it," and he stopped calling.

◆

All of a sudden, in the summer of 1986, I had come to the end of my careful preparation for a professional life and actually entered one. I was excited. And nervous.

I had never lived in New York City and I was anxious about how I would do at Salomon. I wasn't a numbers whiz, and my perception of my abilities was different from that of the recruiters at Yale, who thought I was an ideal Salomon candidate. I felt I was not as strong as the other people entering the firm along with me, to say nothing of those who were already entrenched in the company. Many were, just as I had been told, "the best and the brightest," and I thought from the outset that I—good but not best, smart but not brightest—would quickly be found out. I wasn't the "rising young star" the media dubbed me after the attack, I was just a young woman with a slightly different background from that of my colleagues. That I was a woman in a man's world (there were others in my class and more senior women in the firm) wasn't an issue. My competition, as always, was with myself.

As new associates, we were supposed to learn about many parts of the company's operations during a one-year period. I started in the well-known four-month training class, described in Michael Lewis's book *Liar's Poker*. There were about 150 of us "freshmen," 30 of whom, myself included, would go on to Corporate Finance, the rest to Sales and Trading and Research. In the fifth month, those in Corporate Finance were put into what Salomon called the Generalist Pool, and each morning our supervisor would come to the pool and say, "I need you to work on X project." I'd spend time on that project for as long as necessary, then be thrown back in the pool to await the next assignment.

During the classes, many of the new hires paid little or no attention, but I, of course, took copious notes and often went over them when I got home. I made friends with Michael Allen, who was headed for Sales and Trading, and he used to tease me about my diligence, asking if I wouldn't be happier copying his notes—he took few if any. Michael and I remained friends. It was he who asked me if I was free for dinner the night of the assault. His was the last voice I remembered for over five weeks.

◆

I was having fun. Learning a lot. Busy and productive. "What about development economics, working with the third world?" Mom asked during one of my calls home. It was still too early for that. "This isn't going to last forever," I said to myself about my investment banking life, "but you know what? I'm enjoying it for now."

I was caught up in twelve-to-fourteen-hour days at work. A few clients asked for me to be made part of their team. I gave little thought to what lay ahead, yet I remember looking around at the more senior people and wondering, "Are they doing what I want to be doing?" The answer came back: "I don't think so." I had to *work* at Corporate Finance, it didn't come naturally to me. "That's not going to be me; banking's not how I define myself," I thought. But I didn't know what I wanted, so I kept going.

I can't say I didn't think about the money—it was a tangible reward for hard work and I worked hard. But earning it meant not having much of a life outside the office, and I began to see that for many of my colleagues, money was all-important. It simply wasn't for me. I loved the road shows for IPOs (initial public offerings), when my team would travel to other cities, both in the United States and abroad, convincing institutions to invest in companies that were offering their stock for sale for the first time. These trips, which among other things enabled me to explore and run in new places (running clothes were invariably the first items I packed), were stimulating and exciting. But I felt vaguely unfulfilled, vaguely dissatisfied, to a point where my friends would say, "Don't you think your skills would be better used if you were in a different industry?"

At Salomon, if you weren't promoted to vice president after three years, you'd better look for another job. Thus I determined I'd *make* vice president, not so much because I wanted to climb the Salomon ladder, but because a vice presidency was a new challenge and would look good on my résumé when I wanted to work someplace else. Where? Who knew. I wasn't consciously searching for a job I felt passionate for, but I know now that a quest for different work was an undercurrent, not to rise to the surface for many years.

After a year in New York, I needed a new roommate. My first moved into her own apartment. At the same time, my colleague Pat Garrett's roommate had left to get married. Ideal. Pat and I shared an apartment for eighteen months in a totally platonic fashion. If anything, he worked harder than I did, so we saw each other more at work than we did at home. I found out later that Pat's lustful colleagues wanted to know if he had seen me naked—men! The answer was no. But the arrangement was unsatisfactory for two reasons: first, I wanted a place of my own; and second, I had a new secret. Because it seemed that I was *always* at work, my romantic interests would naturally lie there too. I had started dating Paul Raphael, a Salomon coworker, and since Salomon frowned on intracompany affairs, we didn't want anybody to know.

Paul had his own apartment and never came over to Pat's and mine. He was Lebanese, bright, funny, a good athlete—we would run and bike together—and we shared a fascination with New York, exploring the city on weekends. I was crazy about him, but couldn't show it at work. Indeed, he and I shared an office with another worker who was dumbfounded when, after Paul and I split up, we told him what had been going on around him.

When Paul broke up with me, I felt empty. Luckily, he moved to another department on a different floor at Salomon, but still it was a sad thing; his nearness made going to work tense and stressful. Whenever I saw him, my heart dropped. This was the first man I truly loved.

Living with Pat became more difficult, since several months

after Paul and I parted I began going out with Kevin O'Reilly, a vice president on the equity syndicate desk, again a secret! I thought, "This is ridiculous, all this hiding," and began a search for an apartment of my own. Kevin was a runner and tennis player. It was great fun being with him, but we had no major expectations and did not look at our relationship as potentially long-lasting or profound. Days before the attack, we had a conversation about the direction our relationship was going and wondered whether maybe it was time to end it.

We took up the discussion six months later when I was on a weekend trip away from the rehabilitation hospital and we spent a day together on the New Jersey shore.

❖

April 1989. Like most people my age—twenty-eight—I wasn't given to reflections on the meaning of life or the path on which I was traveling or, in my specific case, the origins of my discontent. I had made many friends, traveled to wonderful places, lived a life most of my contemporaries would envy.

I remember running by myself, heading south in Central Park one rainy night, looking at the lights of the Empire State Building in the distance, relishing the solitude and a feeling of ownership—it was *my* park. I belonged in the city spread out before me—it was *my* city. Running alone in the park, I was taking a risk few others would dare, though I doubt I realized this so concretely; I had conquered challenges at work and made my body strong. I was indestructible, omnipotent. *Comfortable.*

I could run and run and nothing and no one could harm me.

Chapter Three

Life Interrupted

AMBULANCE CALL REPORT

4/20/89 2:29 A.M.

Unknown White Female

Presumptive Diagnosis: Multiple Trauma CNS (Central Nervous System)

Hypothermia.

Patient Condition: Critical

Patient found by Basic Life Support unit in ravine in Central Park laying prone with airway compromise respirations.

Apparent left skull fracture with multiple deep lacerations
noted, edema left eye noted, contusions & abrasions noted
on lower extremities and torso. Patient clad only in "jogging"
bra, extremely hypothermic with mud and water all over body
and head, slight decortication at scene, airway compromise
noted after rescue due to facial edema. Patient intubated and
hyperventilated en route to hospital.

The report—understated, blunt, chilling in its matter-of-factness—takes my breath away. Five gashes had split my scalp open; my face was covered with blood. I had been beaten beyond recognition. I was bruised on every part of my body except the soles of my feet. My skin was purple and black, and my left eye was not where it should have been. The admitting physician feared for my life. My brother Bill's thought when he first saw me in the ICU summed up the reactions of all those closest to me: "This is not Trisha."*

My badly bruised and battered body with a head swelled to twice its normal size lay comatose in that hospital room. During that missing time, I almost died, was put on a ventilator and taken off, had my eye rebuilt, and was started back toward health, while doctors and family, friends and strangers, wondered and worried about how much mental and physical capacity, how much of *me*, would return. But if we define ourselves by our consciousness, our awareness, then for more than five weeks I was not there. There *was* no Trisha Meili.

I've read a lot about those weeks in newspaper clippings and

---

*My friend Ken said that only when he noticed my "tiny, straight nose" did he
believe I was the person in the bed.

medical reports, and my doctors and my family have told me what my condition was. It's eerie to learn of events playing out around me then, of words I spoke. It's as though there's a hole in my existence into which I'd fallen and on my return can never fill. I will never fully understand what my family, friends, the city, even the entire country, went through. They will never understand what I experienced, the darkness and the unknown.

I had mixed feelings about exploring that time more deeply. My reluctance stemmed from wanting to keep myself removed from the full extent of what was done to me and what was needed, medically, to keep me alive. I didn't want it to become too real. It's why I wouldn't look at pictures of my battered self and why, when I read the reports and heard the stories, I remained detached. The accounts seemed like a description of someone else, someone who might not have recovered, and I didn't read too carefully, listen too closely. Yet I live with the real consequences of the attack every day.

But while my detachment might have saved me then, those seven weeks are crucial in the making of the person I am today. I knew I must investigate them further. I wanted to get a true sense of what my primary caregivers—doctors, nurses, therapists—were thinking and feeling as they helped restore me, even as I lay in a coma, completely unaware of their efforts. How badly off was I? How deep and how dark was the hole?

Thus, with considerable fear, in May 2002 I decided to go back down into the hole, this time with my eyes and ears and feelings alert. A visit with Dr. Kurtz, the chief of the cadre of doctors who attended me at Metropolitan, is where I decided to start.

I open the door of his outer office. There he is.

"You look *terrific!*" He hugs me with the warmth of a parent welcoming a long-lost daughter, and now he holds me at arm's length; studies my face. A genial man with thinning hair and only a bit more girth than he had at Metropolitan during my stay there, his eyes are bright with pleasure, and he summons a doctor who works with him, his secretary, and another assistant, introducing me to them as if he were a sculptor and I his masterpiece.

I feel honored. Dr. Kurtz had kindly visited me twice at the rehabilitation hospital after I was transferred there, and he and I have had lunch a few times during the ensuing years, pleasant meetings without significant emotional weight. I did meet with him in the winter of 1990 to go through my hospital records. Huge volumes sat on his desk and he started a page-by-page chronological recounting of what had happened. But there was too much technical information, and I couldn't focus on it; maybe I wasn't ready to hear it, either cognitively or emotionally. Today he knows I am in his office to learn in layman's terms the details of the start of my recovery, for I am going public, writing a book.

He leads me into his inner office and shuts the door. We are on the third floor of Kings County Hospital in Brooklyn, where Dr. Kurtz has been codirector of Trauma and Surgical Critical Care since 1999—"a better position and better pay," he explains. (At Metropolitan he was director of the Surgical Intensive Care Unit.) I notice that on the wall to the right of his desk are two framed front pages of newspapers, one from the May 2, 1989, *Newsday*, which shows him with his hands raised in triumph under the headline "Jogger's Doc: She Gave a High Five," the other from the May 4 edition of the *New York Post* picturing him holding up two flash cards—YES and NO—under the headline "Answered Prayers."

The pictures startle me. Once again I am in that strange place where my sense of self—an ordinary, modest, private person—runs head-on into the fact that as the Central Park Jogger I've become extraordinary. Thinking earlier about the thousands of letters, messages, and gifts that were sent to me, I'd ask myself, "If the situation were reversed, would *I* write a letter or send a keepsake to someone I didn't know?" "You can't know the answer unless you were in that circumstance" is the easy response, but I think, "I probably wouldn't have done that." Maybe it's those people who would do that, who *did* do that, who are the extraordinary ones. Maybe we are all ordinary and extraordinary at once. There's a touch of Dr. Kurtz's self-pride in the pictures. I'm pleased he considers his work on my case so special.

He tells me that on April 20 he was called early in the morning by Dr. Isaac Sapozhnikov, the ER physician on duty. When he got to the hospital, he took over my care until I left Metropolitan seven weeks later. "I saw the heavy beating you had. Wounds on your head, one of which persists as a scar right until today. Lacerations and avulsions—like tearing off part of the skin. There were at least four of them on the left and one on the right."

His voice is emotionless, and I feel little emotion of my own. While far more comprehensible than the reports I've read, and far more human, to me it's still an impersonal diagnosis to a patient. It's as though it's 1990 and we're going through the reports again. I know we have a deep bond. I've felt it strongly over the years. But so far I'm as detached from his spoken information as I was from the written reports.

He doesn't know what caused the cuts, he tells me. Maybe a broken bottle or a jagged piece of glass. And, he believes, a brick or a rock had crushed my eye socket. "Your temperature was eighty-five F, a condition laymen call exposure. In itself, it can cause death if not treated. Too, you had a blood pressure which was seventy systolic, and the ER people couldn't hear or feel the diastolic rhythm. We would call that a Class 4 hemorrhagic shock—the most profound form of shock. It took at least three-quarters of the complement of red blood cells to restore you to something approaching normal—enough to be acceptable. At the time I said you had something like seventy-five to eighty percent blood volume loss. When people bleed to death, they don't really bleed out every last drop of blood in their body, because by the time they get to the level you were at, the loss of blood means there won't be enough blood to keep the heart beating and that's the end of life. You weighed about a hundred pounds soaking wet, so that amount of blood loss . . ."

For a moment, he drops his professional veneer and smiles. "It was pretty amazing, as I thought then and still think now, that your heart was still pumping away. I think part of the credit for that goes to the fact that you were in excellent athletic condition"—another smile—"and you're an indomitable person. You were in a situation where other people like you might well be dead—and you weren't."

Ironic, I think. I might have been in "excellent athletic condition," but I still wasn't eating well. I wonder how my body survived, and it starts to sink in that maybe the answer lies in what

Dr. Kurtz called "indomitable spirit," something that can't be defined in medical terms. The phrase sounds strange coming from a scientist, and perhaps that's why it resonates strongly in me. Others have called me "indomitable," but it's not an image I've ever had of myself. Now I think, *Maybe.* Even in the coma I was apparently goddamned if I was going to die. Dr. Kurtz is looking at me with affection. I am eager for him to go on, for I feel a more personal connection. Not only with him, but with *me*—the me I was immediately after the attack.

When patients are brought to the ER as close to death as I was, he explains, doctors' first concerns are the "ABC's"—Airway (I was intubated even in the ambulance); Breathing (I was hooked up to a ventilator); and Circulation (blood had to be restored and sent flowing to the heart so it could pump). In my case, along with the ABC's, a simultaneous threat was that excessive swelling in my brain would cause an increase of the pressure of the brain against the skull. That, combined with the loss of blood pressure, might lead to anoxia, the inability of oxygen to get to the brain. The possible result was a brain function so damaged it could not support a quality of existence worthy of being called a life. "And so," he says, "your intracranial pressure was monitored with a slang bolt attached to your skull." My brother Bill referred to it as my "spark plug."

"They evaluated you on a neurological scale—they call it a Glasgow Coma Scale—which rates a patient's neurologic response on a three-to-fifteen level. Fifteen indicates normal consciousness and brain function: fully alert, awake, responsive. And three is what you get for just being alive: totally unresponsive. The score is evaluated according to your eye responses, your verbal responses, and your motor responses. Up to four for eye responses, up to five for verbal responses, and up to six for motor—fifteen." He pauses. "In total, you were a four—four to five."

I'd already talked to Dr. Kurtz about this when I went back to Metropolitan to read the medical reports. While the cold figures were, as he gently confirmed then, vivid evidence of just how close to death I'd been, my protection then had been to intellectualize it, not *feel* it. When I hear it from him today, I'm struck by how scary it is, how amazing. *Four to five.* The hole had been deep.

"And my eye was smashed in?" It is a key question, for I still have double vision when I've worked too long or am tired. And I'm squeamish about eyes. Was I squeamish before the attack? I don't remember, but it sure didn't make the squeamishness better. I never liked watching violent movies and didn't want to become a vet or a doctor because it meant having to perform surgery. I did watch football games, but now it makes me uncomfortable when the players get hit in the head, especially if television shows a slow-motion replay. And I absolutely can't watch a prizefight; the potential consequences are too real for me.

"You had a bad orbital blowout fracture. It wasn't a penetrating instrument that hit you in the eye or you would have lost the eyeball. Anyway, your orbital rim and the cheekbone and the zygoma—the bone that connects the cheekbone and goes back toward the ear—were fractured at the point where they come together. The result was that the cheek looked as if it were pushed in permanently, and it would have made you look much more homely than you are."

Again he smiles, fondly I think, to show me he's making a backhanded compliment. He's enjoying telling me the details, but I haven't enjoyed listening to them. Part of me wants to know, but part definitely doesn't. I want to understand if what I went through was indeed horrific, yet I squirm from the details. It's confusing. Dr. Marilee Sipski, my attending physician at Gaylord, the rehabilitation hospital I was sent to after Metropolitan, told me that when I got there, I wanted to know everything about what had happened and we went through the Metropolitan Hospital progress reports together. But I can't remember this. That early on, the black hole did not give up any of its secrets.

"The force of the blow was such that it pushed your eyeball back," Dr. Kurtz says. "The eyeball is filled with liquid. Liquid is not compressible, so any force transmitted to the surface of the eyeball will be transmitted to the back of the eyeball too. And that caused the eyeball to explode to the very thin plates of the orbital floor, plates that are almost paper-thin. They normally delicately suspend the eyeball so that it can be pulled this way and that by the different muscles that are attached to it—six muscles attached to each eyeball. Those are what move your eyeball around, but you couldn't move your eyeball because the muscles were entrapped in the orbital floor."

"It's astonishing that anybody was able to put my face back together again," I say.

"Yeah, well, it took some pretty fancy surgery. You had an excellent ophthalmic surgeon, Bob Della Rocca. You still see a little double, I'll bet. Even with a master surgeon at the top of his ability, it's sometimes impossible to get it aligned exactly the way it had been before. Considering the damage, I think he did a great job."

"Great job" barely begins to describe it. When I look in the mirror and see my face, my familiar face, only a tiny scar reminds me that there might have been no eye at all. I can picture myself before the attack and I see myself now. But I have no mental image of the left side of my face smashed in. I was spared. It accounts for some of my confusion over the severity of my injuries. Yes, I'm willing to revisit facts, but to see pictures? Just too hard. Too horrible.

"When you first saw me, did you think I'd survive?" I ask.

"Less than fifty percent," he admits. "Still, I thought you had a chance, mostly because you were young. The ultimate survival issue we took care of pretty quickly; within a few hours we figured you'd live.* After that, it was a question of whether you'd recover your normal brain function—here too I thought you had less than a 50 percent chance—and that we made sure nobody made any stupid mistakes while you were in the ICU on a ventilator with your life, literally, hanging by a thread. Your brain and kidneys weren't working—we had to be your brain and your kidneys for you. We had numbers of talented and capable people there, but they are human beings and human awareness sometimes lapses and people are looking in the other direction when tubes come out that shouldn't come out. None of this happened with you, but I wanted to make damn sure it didn't happen, which is why I didn't take off any days while you were in the hospital. I saw you every day, and at the very critical days I sat with you in the room and I literally watched every monitor to make sure there weren't any mistakes made."

He didn't take off any days while I was there! I'm convinced

---

*Still, my family describe April 20 as a time of despair; they had the sense that I was already gone. In a family conference that afternoon, Dr. Kurtz indicated that my chances for life were 50 percent and that severe brain damage was likely.

that his presence by my side—his will matched with mine—
made a difference. He had been talking calmly about medical
marvels, but now, when he speaks of the bond he felt with me, I
sense his deep emotion. He had once told me the reason. I wonder if he will bring it up again.

"You had been raped," he says.

"Was there damage or—"

"No. I mean, there was semen present in your genital tract,
but no physical damage. The vagina is meant to have sexual
intercourse, and it's evolved so it can do it. Think of prostitutes
who have ten customers a night. The mere act of penile pene-
tration does spiritual damage to the woman, but not physical
unless you have some kind of maniac who uses foreign objects
or an adult male attacking a child." He is speaking intensely now,
his face red, his tone angry. "A lot of people think that if there
was no damage, there was no rape or it's not such a bad deal.
That's untrue. This is a violent, forced act against the wishes of
the woman. We know you were raped because we found visible
semen in your genital tract. Even the CAT scan of your
abdomen showed fluid filling the uterus."

This was familiar ground to me; the prosecutor, Elizabeth
Lederer, had explained it. Thus I was able to listen with relative
calmness. Dr. Kurtz tells me I'm fortunate to have no memory of
the rape, and I know he's right. It probably kept me sane. On the
other hand, it troubles me not to know what happened.

The whole question of what other things I don't remember—
events unrelated to the attack—has plagued me for fourteen
years. To have vivid memories and blank spaces makes me question my memory again and again. Is the inability to remember a
name, say, or a word or a fact or a face attack-related?

"I know loss of memory is common with brain injury. Did you suspect I'd have no memory of the attack?" I ask.

"With severe brain injury, absolutely. It's universal. It's not like the movies of war veterans who come back with amnesia and twenty years later remember who their wife was and recover their lives. Each memory is implanted, initially as a result of an electrical phenomenon, and then after a few days it gets chemically imprinted on the brain cells, the latter being the more permanent memory storage, the electrical one being transient. Brain traumas—blows, then subsequent poor oxygenation of the brain—result in the wiping out of the recorded electrical impulses. So I was confident then, and I'm confident now, that you'll never have a biological memory of the attack, the electrical moment never made it to the brain cells. You had acute brain dysfunction from the trauma, which accounts for the long void in your memory after the attack."

He tells me that a hospital policeman, anxious for his fifteen minutes of fame, had told the *New York Post* that I remembered the assault and could identify the rapists, and he laughs at the preposterousness of it. "You're in the strange position of having this widely publicized and having heard or seen feedback of it for thirteen years. You've surely become deeply immersed in it, but not from your own memory." He looks at me sympathetically. "I've tried to imagine how you must feel hearing all these discussions of what you did and said and looked like and what happened to you. I mean, if you weren't as strong a person, this could drive you to drink."

He takes me through my gradual recovery: how, on the second try, they were able to take me off the ventilator; how my Glasgow Coma Scale gradually came up; how, in fits and starts—

the squeeze of a hand, the smile at a familiar face, the nod in answer to a question—I came out of the coma. Technically, you're out of a coma when your Glasgow Coma Scale reaches eight, he tells me. But "you're not really normal until you're 'normal'—a fifteen on the Glasgow Coma Scale. Until then, amnesia is likely."

At first, my verbal responses were incoherent nonsense, but gradually I oriented to day and time and was able to read the YES and NO flash cards he was holding in the photograph. My progress was uneven; there was backsliding, a one-day temperature of 106, pneumonia, good hours followed by bad. But my condition was improving.

"One more thing," I said. "I heard that I was restrained, basically tied to the bed because I was thrashing about a lot and potentially yanking tubes out. Is that true, and is that what led to getting the private nurses?"

"Thrashing's very common, virtually universal with patients with severe brain injuries. At a stage when you no longer need IVs or oxygen, it doesn't matter too much. But you did need those things and you could have pulled the lines out, and we didn't want to sedate you enough to knock you out because doing that would suppress your cough and gag reflexes, so we did physically restrain you. And, no, we didn't get the private nurses in so the restraints could be removed, but for whatever immediate help they could give you."

My daytime private nurse was Patricia Babb, who stayed with me the entire time at Metropolitan and for several weeks at Gaylord. I had made an appointment to see her a few days after this meeting with Dr. Kurtz, and I became more and more eager to hear her recollections as I listened to him.

"I agreed to the private nurses because they could do all those little extra things for you," Dr. Kurtz continues, "massaging you, applying lotions, getting you into and out of bed, things like that. It was the right thing to do under the circumstances. It helped you. I don't know that it helped change the outcome, but it probably gave you physically more comfort and it certainly gave your parents comfort. I always knew I had extra people keeping a hawk eye on you."

What he says adds to my conviction that physical touch, an atmosphere of goodwill, family, friends, and even strangers rooting for you—all these help in recovery. That my parents were comforted, for example, surely helped them comfort me.

"Tell me about your own feelings through all of this," I say.

He pauses, reflecting. "I wind up, despite having lots of patients going through what you did and even worse kinds of troubles, identifying with them to a certain extent. If they're from completely different backgrounds, it's more of a stretch, but though you don't have the same religious background, professionally, educationally . . ."

Fluid and articulate until now, he is having trouble putting his feelings into words, though his demeanor remains the same. His voice lowers. "You're the kind of person I might have turned into if I had gone into business. You had a couple of concerned, loving parents, like my own parents were. When I saw you, I thought, 'Here's a beautiful life. I want to make sure she gets it back.' " He hesitates. "I think my residents would be amazed to see I have this much emotion."

We have arrived at a new, more profound place. I know doctors *must* remain detached, otherwise they'd go mad.

"You know," he says, "your case was volatile from an entirely

different point of view too. The suspects were all black or Hispanic. And a lot of members of the black community saw this as
a hostile attack on them—you know, an effort by the white man
to pin a rape on blacks."

"Yes."

"As someone who's steeped himself deeply in black history, I
knew where they were coming from. Obviously I'm not black
myself, but my wife is black and I have a lot of sympathy for
people who may have been unjustly accused. But as a physician,
I view myself as an advocate of the patient, always taking care of
the medical wounds. At the trials, I told the truth as I saw it, I
told what had happened to you. I described the brutality of your
injuries, of how you were so close to death. The fact is that if you
hadn't been brought to us, a place that was skilled in trauma
care, you quickly would have been dead."

His eyes grow teary, and he does not look at me. I reach out
to touch his arm.

"I also had one other person in a circumstance that made me
feel particularly sensitive to what happened to you. My oldest
daughter, Holly, was raped on the street at gunpoint just one
month before you were attacked." He wipes his eyes, takes a
breath. "Anyway, that sort of is the background to your case."

There is a moment's silence before he returns to the story of
my physical care. He mentions a talented neurosurgeon, Dr. Kent
Duffy; an ear, nose, and throat specialist, Dr. William Levin; Dr.
Mary Ann Cohen, my psychiatrist; and others who were instrumental in my recovery at Metropolitan. I am viscerally aware
of—stunned by—the *scope* of all that was done, what was
involved in terms of doctors, nurses, and therapists. I know that in
other cases as catastrophic as mine the same team, or one like it,

would be assembled. Yet sitting next to the man who had literally saved my life, I am overwhelmed that, moments ago, he opened himself up enough for me to offer him some comfort in return.

"The ending of amnesia, which is different from emerging from a coma, is also a slow process," he tells me in summation. "But you went from not remembering anything to remembering lots of things. Most people reassemble reality in a more fragmentary fashion than you did."

I'm pleased that's his recollection; it's mine too. "It was the Friday of Memorial Day weekend that I started to remember something happening," I say. "I remember telling my former boyfriend to shut up. And I interacted with my brothers in a real way. My brother Steve said to me that I just 'changed' that weekend—and called my parents so they could hear me talk like my old self. It was that I was once again the real me, and he remembers calling a friend and saying, 'She's back!'"

Dr. Kurtz nods. "Yeah. Well, that's what happened. It was like night and day. That was Friday of Memorial Day weekend, and twelve days later you were out of Metropolitan."

"Right. To Gaylord, my next hospital. I remember waving good-bye to you from the ambulance."

There is one more comment from Dr. Kurtz, a reiteration of his rage at the brutality of the crime. "The essential thing is you were almost destroyed—almost killed—and for no good reason. It's lucky for you that you don't remember the assault. But you've got to live with the aftereffects for the rest of your life, this extraordinary crime, this violence. That's the part that bothers me more than the rape."

It is a rant against injustice from a distance of thirteen years, an anger that I have never felt, and I recognize the same anger my family expressed. But my anger is different—it's not so much *How could you do this to me?* but *How could you do this to my family?* My feeling was always that I would be essentially okay, though I knew I would have to live with the consequences, mentally, physically, and psychologically. But my *family*; they were really suffering. Today I add, *How could you do this to Dr. Kurtz?*

We stand. Dr. Kurtz leads me back to his outer office where we say good-bye. After all these years, the extent of just how bad the assault was is finally sinking in. I feel it in my body, not the sensations of being attacked, but the impact of the attack, the aftermath, and I am more than thankful for his care. I've had conversations about my treatment before, with Dr. Kurtz and others, but today his explanation and his emotion have penetrated my soul.

◆

Six days after my visit with Dr. Kurtz, I arrive at the home of Pat Babb. A strong, solid woman, she lives in the Midwood section of Brooklyn, in an apartment jammed with artifacts from Trinidad, her birthplace, from England, where she received her nurse's training, and from New York City, where she has lived much of her life. She is sixty now, about to retire and move to Atlanta to be with the rest of her family. We've corresponded and spoken with each other from time to time over the years, and she's remained friends with my aunt Barbara from the moment they met at my bedside. She was with me during the transition between Metropolitan and Gaylord. Hers is a face I know well.

She hugs me warmly, and we sit at her dining room table. She tells me that she was called to my case by the Health and Hospitals Corporation, which maintained an agency of private nurses: There is a woman at Metropolitan Hospital who needs personalized care because, though unconscious, she is very agitated. On April 22, Pat came to the hospital, ready for battle.

"You were bruised and they had you tied to the bed," she says heatedly. "But I'm a hands-on nurse. You don't hurt patients, you do everything possible to ease their transition from illness into health. So I immediately untied you because you were fighting the restraints, and it seemed to me you were reliving the attack over and over. I told you, 'You're safe. It's over. You're not there anymore. You're safe now.'

"You're very small, and as you can see, I'm very strong, so my way of restraining you was to pick you up and hold you. Everybody watching was amazed. But you had regressed, and to me, when a child needs comforting, you're supposed to hold her. There was also a special bed which you could put water in, and I would use warm water to bathe you. That put you to sleep. When I was there—we worked twelve-hour shifts; you had another nurse, Joy, a blond lady, very nice—I threw everybody out of the room. Your visitors didn't like it, but you're unconscious. What good were they doing you? To me, everything that's happening to a sick person should be for her benefit, not for the people around her. I wasn't there to take care of them, I was there to take care of you. Your brother Steve called me The General."

We laugh. "Eventually you got to like that feel. You got to trust it. You got to like my voice, even when you were unconscious. 'It's me,' I'd say. 'Calm down. Everything's all right.' And you would calm down. The doctors couldn't understand how I could calm you, because I think they weren't listening to you. Patients know what's happening to them even when they're in pain or unconscious, even when it's something that the patient didn't know. I figured, 'This girl is reliving the situation over and over, over and over. If we can stop her from doing this, she'll be fine.' So I talked to you in a calm voice and held you in a nurturing way, and you felt a difference in the holding and responded to that. The psychiatrist asked, 'How do you do that?' and she would come and watch me."

I'm struck by her brand of nurturing, how lucky I was, but then I remember my conversation with Dr. Kurtz. "A doctor would say the thrashing was a neurological reaction," I say.

"You were fighting for your life! That's why the cursing came out. Of course I couldn't hear the cursing when you were on the ventilator, but when you were extubated, the words came out." She grins. "You have a large vocabulary." The thought of my mother's expression if she had heard my uninhibited cursing— an involuntary aftereffect of many head injuries—makes me laugh.

Was Pat right about the fight for life? I wonder. My knuckles were bruised after the attack, so I probably did. There are times when, before I go to sleep, I envision what the attack must have been like and how I must have been scared out of my mind. I'll even think about the actual beating and how it must have felt. But I haven't woken up after a bad dream feeling that or thinking someone's coming to get me. If the thrashing was a reenactment, why haven't I unconsciously reenacted the attack since? I believe Dr. Kurtz's view that there is no biological memory of the attack, nothing to relive. But Pat's nurturing touch and calm voice did quiet my agitation. I responded physiologically and her care helped reduce the stress from the trauma.

"You know," she says, "I felt you weren't cognitively impaired even though everybody else thought you were."

What hope she must have given my family! "What made you think so?"

"Well, I've had a lot of experience with sick people, and I knew that even though you couldn't speak, as soon as I calmed you down, if I asked you to hold my hand or try to turn over, you did it."

Pat, it seems, had her own Glasgow Coma Scale.

"I'm a registered nurse, but I've done alternative therapies and I believe in them," she continues. "People from all over the world were sending you oils and waters, and to me the thing is, if it don't hurt, it might help! So I would bathe you and rub you from head to foot with those oils. And I brought relaxation tapes from home and would play them for you. Cards came in from all over the world, and I spent hours reading them to you. I tried to pick ones from different countries, different parts of America, from different races, so you would know. Children wrote poems. There were stuffed animals up the kazoo, and flowers, flowers. We sent them to children's hospitals. Relics from Lourdes, water from Russia and Germany. Catholics sent, Jews sent, and Muslims sent. Everybody sent according to what they believed their God to be. And soon—I can't remember how many days it was—you got conscious."

She tells me that soon she came in every day, sensing that I'd regress when she wasn't there. "I didn't want any of the bad things the doctors said might happen to happen. It's important to stay on key, to stay focused, because you can't be going back, you have to be going forward." She looks at me intently. "I think nothing happens by accident. I was the one who was supposed to take care of you."

I'm not sure I share her philosophy, but there's no denying that her nurturing was vital, and maybe she's right—maybe she *was* "supposed" to have a role in my recovery.

"This is a beautiful country," she continues, "but a lot of things happen here that are not beautiful. You happened to be caught up in one of the not-beautiful things, but you were a beautiful person. I don't think people are in the wrong place at any wrong time—they have a right to be where they want to be anytime they want to be. And I'm just sorry you weren't big enough to punch anyone's lights out."

"I tried," I say sheepishly.

"I know. Oh, boy, when you were unconscious, the fighting you did! And one more thing: I'm a black person, and if it was black people who hurt you, I guess it was supposed to be a black person to get you back. Some black hospital nurses were afraid of you because supposedly somebody black had hurt you. Some didn't want to touch you. They figured anything they'd do would be scrutinized. But you were a patient. No matter what color, what size, what race—the patient's sick. The majority of people in the world—rich, poor, and in between—have good intentions."

I asked Pat how she got along with my family.

She was fond of my brothers—she referred to Bill as "the Mayor"—felt an immediate kinship with my aunt Barbara, and kept saying to my parents that I'd be fine. Her conviction gave them hope. Mom and Dad had a lot of respect for Pat's judgment and how she took care of me; they saw the difference it made. I'm sure that's why they wanted Pat to accompany me to Gaylord, where she could be a calming presence during my transition to a new hospital. No one knew how I'd respond.

The doctors made her mad. If I was asleep when they came to check on me, she wouldn't let them wake me to find out how I was. "You needed sleep. To me, when you were sleeping, that was gold. I didn't care who came, and they would come at any time. You were getting tube feeding, and it caused a lot of diarrhea. I would just clean you and you'd have diarrhea again. You'd be soiled and they'd walk into the room and expect to interview you. Now, who's this for? So then I'd say, 'No, you gotta leave. I have to take care of her *now*. You let me finish, then you come back.'"

She is fierce now, reliving. "There was another thing I thought shouldn't be done, those physicians talking about your condition or problems around your bed. I thought they should go to a conference room, because I thought you knew what they were saying. You might not be able to talk, but you could hear. Nothing was wrong with your ears. And besides, what's the point of saying she can't or she'll never or she won't. You were going to believe them. So as soon as they left, I said, 'Don't pay them any mind. What do they know? You're a hero. You're a trouper.' And when you began to talk, I'd say, 'Who's the captain of the ship?' and you'd say, 'I am!' And I'd say, 'You're the captain here. Nobody else is my boss. You can do anything you want.'"

I think, God, that's perfect! Just the right tack, and I laugh. "You were bossy."

"Very. But sometimes it's not bossy, it's directional. After the operation, one side of your face drooped, you know, where the injury was done. You still drooled a little and that made them think there was something wrong with your brain, but I thought you just had to get adjusted. So I told you, 'You're not to do that. It's not acceptable.'

"I'd say, 'Trisha, today is Monday. By Wednesday, you're going to do such and such.' And you were a worker. Although we're from totally different backgrounds, we have the same mind-set. We set goals and we achieve goals. We started with the song "Itsy-Bitsy Spider." Every week we did something else, and we did more. I remember your friend Ken. He was amazed. You and I would do the crossword. He said, 'I can't believe you can do this,' but it was our job every morning. And in ink. That way you can't cheat."

She grins. "And we walked. They said you wouldn't walk. In fact, they left us alone a lot, which was good, because I would walk you by myself. At first we had a walker, but I didn't want you to use it. So I would support you, first a quarter way down the corridor, then halfway, then full way."*

We're in the flow of it, and the dialogue comes easily. "By the time I went to Gaylord," I say, "I was starting to remember things, and so I had a sense that 'I've got to work but it's going to be okay.' I actually thought I was in relatively good shape, other than the fact I couldn't walk."

"I thought you were in good shape and I thought you *would* walk. Some said, 'Oh, she'll limp.' But I thought you'd walk

---

*Actually, my physical therapy started on my fifth day at Metropolitan, while I was still in a coma. My arms and legs were stretched. I was raised to sit at a forty-five-degree angle and made to cough to clear my lungs. I was moved from side to side, made to lie on my stomach, and later I was taught to stay on my hands and knees so I could get used to bearing my own weight. Eventually, these exercises, performed in five-to-ten minute sessions, led to sitting by myself and walking with assistance.

without a limp because there was nothing wrong with your legs. Nothing wrong with your spine."

I remember that at one point I asked Pat when she thought I'd walk again, and she said I'd be walking in two weeks. But it took three weeks, and I thought, "Oh, I'm going to disappoint Pat." She admits she told me it would take less time than she thought on the theory that, even with children, if you let them feel they can do more than they can, they'll do more than you expect.

Did her prodding, her belief that I'd get completely well, help as much as the actual work? Again, I'm sure it played a part. Pat drove me, I knew, no harder than I drove myself. She was right: we had the same mind-set.

We talk briefly about the time at Gaylord, where Pat "sat around and grew fat" because, since I had a full day's schedule of therapies and progressed well, she had little to do. Then we stand and hug good-bye. As I'm leaving, Pat says, "Before you could speak, your aunt Barbara said to me, 'Do you think that Trisha will remember any of this?' I said, 'I doubt it. Most patients don't.' And she said, 'Do you think she'll remember *you*?' I said, 'I don't think she will.' Barbara said, 'I'll make sure she does.'"

Yes, I think, I have a sense memory of Pat at Metropolitan; she is in my bloodstream. And I say, "I wasn't going to forget you. Ever."

◆

If any more proof were needed that both mind and body are essential in healing, Pat provided it. I leave her home filled with gratitude that so empathic and protective a person was on my side. Her gentle touch supplied safety. Her insistence on setting goals and achieving them provided just the impetus needed to force me forward. This was the power of touch, the power of doing.

As I take the train home that evening, I think how fortunate I am to have had Kurtz and Babb as my healers. I take a deep breath and wonder how it all happened; indeed, I'm so thankful I want to cry. Then the conductor announces my stop, and I am no longer in the past but in the present. The result of their work is a blessing. Here I am!

◆

"It's called the technique of running commentary," Dr. Mary Ann Cohen says, describing the work she does with comatose patients, and thus did with me. We are in her office on Central Park West, and while she talks, I study her carefully, for I have no memory of her whatsoever, though she visited me dozens of times at Metropolitan. She is a small, youthful woman—I'm amazed when she tells me she's nearly sixty-one—and I had previously read her progress notes and marveled how I could be so intellectually out of commission, unaware of day, time, place, and identities, and often giving different answers to the same questions asked minutes or hours before. Throughout I thought her name was Victoria, for example, even though she kept reintroducing herself as Mary Ann; I told her my favorite sport was stamp collecting, that I was born in Indianapolis, and that I was seventeen years old.

The technique of running commentary, she explains, is simply to keep talking to the patient in the hope that over days, weeks, months, or even years a connection between therapist and patient will be made and the patient will begin to talk. The natural outcome of a coma is not death but awakening and health, she says, and talk is part of awakening. From my family, she learned that I was an investment banker and a runner, so she talked to me about that, and about Yale and New Haven—"you know, just any old thing that comes to mind."

Her visits, often more than one a day since my condition was so volatile, were twenty minutes at first, then later, when I was out of the coma, up to forty minutes. She asked my family and friends to talk to me, not just sit by my side, and to bring objects from my present and my past—trinkets, posters, stuffed animals, and pictures of themselves or anybody who looked familiar— that they could put around me to serve as cues to bring me back. "I told them to always say who they were and what the place was, the day, the date, the month, the year." From Pat Babb's perspective, this was not particularly effective, at least early on; she thought it was more helpful to my visitors than to me.

Dr. Cohen, like Pat Babb, never doubted that I'd recover, though of course neither saw me when I was first admitted on April 20. "You were pretty battered, but I'm an optimistic person. When I first saw you, in a coma and in need of resuscitation, it didn't look good, but my intuition sensed you were going to be fine. I wasn't sure you could get all your mental function back, but I was positive you'd get most of it."

Like Pat Babb, Dr. Cohen is convinced my thrashing was directly related to the attack. "There was a point when you were in the coma where you would just try to run really fast away from something, and fighting hard. It was like you were reliving what had happened to you. At first I wasn't sure what it was—I couldn't ask you—but it seemed like that's what was happening.

That's another reason I wanted people around you twenty-four/seven."

She praises Pat, remarking on the care she provided and reaffirming my own belief in that profound key to my recovery. "What happened when I started to come out of the coma?" I ask.

"You were delirious, and delirium causes confusion—it's called a syndrome of cerebral insufficiency. The classic sign is fluctuating levels of consciousness, and that's where you were. It also causes fluctuations in emotions, fluctuations in mood. Someone can come in the morning and say, 'Gee, Trisha, you look great today.' And then someone else can come in an hour later and say, 'What's wrong with her? She's so agitated.' It's part of the same process."

Dr. Cohen explains that she checked for levels of alertness, for orientation—whether I knew where I was or who was talking to me, for example. Then there was registration and recall—whether I could repeat three or four words after an interval of distraction. "What did I say to you when I first walked in?" she'd ask me, and I'd try to remember, though often I couldn't. Today, I have no memory of such tests, though my family told me I was asked questions all the time and seemed to resent it. My brother Steve kids me that I would pretend to sleep so I wouldn't have to perform.

Dr. Cohen checked for abstract reasoning as well, whether I could describe the similarities between an airplane and a train ("they're both means of travel") or an orange and an apple ("they're both fruits"). She asked me to spell simple words backward. There were tests of information, tests of current events, logic, and reasoning. And of course there were tests for memory; in my case, recent memory was nonexistent because it had been shattered by the massive trauma. "But you talked clearly about philosophers you had read," Dr. Cohen tells me now, as though to cheer me up.

I'm flabbergasted. I did not read philosophers, never took a philosophy course in school—and we try to puzzle out where my knowledge came from. How could I speak about a topic I have no recollection of learning? It seems strange, another mystery of the mind I shall never fathom.

There were drawing tests as well, one of which I specifically *do* remember, so it was probably given around that eventful Memorial Day weekend. I was asked to draw the face of a clock. I put in the 12 first, then the 6, and then the 3 and the 9, to get the placement right for the other numbers. I was thinking, "This doesn't look too bad," and even though my manual dexterity wasn't great, I was proud of myself. Then the *real* test came: "Draw two o'clock."

I froze. I couldn't remember which was longer, the hour hand or the minute hand. I couldn't admit this, feeling that if I didn't get it right, then I'd be considered stupid. Me, from a family that stressed education. How embarrassing. And then I hit on a solution: I'd make both hands the same size! That way no one would realize my brain was still muddled; I'd fool them all. At that time, the episode made me aware that something was very wrong, and it scared me. *What had happened to my brain?* Years later, when I read the report, it said I had misplaced the hand positioning, so obviously my deception failed. Today, writing about it, I'm fascinated by what it showed of my state of mind. I *wanted* to be well, to be "normal," as early as six weeks after the attack.

Before I leave, I ask Dr. Cohen if we ever talked about the

attack. She says I asked questions about it, but that she was purposely vague when discussing it, primarily because she knew a court case was coming up and she didn't want to influence my thinking—the prosecutor would need my unadulterated testimony. "My role," she said, "was to be with you if you began to remember, help you put those horrible feelings away, be there for you if you were frightened."

When I read her progress reports, I am intrigued by how quickly my mind developed. Until the day before memory began to return, Dr. Cohen noted "delirium" under her impressions and commented on a degree of confusion and disorientation. A few days later, "delirium" no longer appears; I had "made dramatic progress in terms of function and ability to comprehend what happened."

Dr. Cohen's account also noted that I was "coping well with the stress of the attack," though two days later she reported that I had asked, "When will my throat stop hurting and when will my brain start working better?" One week after being labeled delirious, I had the presence of mind to tell her, "I don't know what happened and maybe I will never know, but I know I was attacked and I will just have to accept it and deal with it." Such complex reasoning so soon after the brain injury now seems to me astonishing. Clearly, I had absorbed that I was attacked even when I was at Metropolitan. What I said then I believe still, and I based my recovery, and indeed my postattack life, on those words. The attack happened. I accept that it happened and that it changed my life. And I've dealt with it in different ways in the years that followed.

◆

Though I feel little connection with Dr. Cohen—nothing like the bond with Dr. Kurtz or Pat Babb—again I'm amazed by further evidence of the extraordinary support I was given at Metropolitan. I ask her a question that had begun to haunt me: "What if a person was attacked the way I was attacked but didn't get the care you gave me and my family gave me and the doctors and nurses gave me? Is the likelihood that she would not recover or recover as well?"

The answer comes quickly: "Right."

"So the brain's not self-healing? I mean, it needs a push?"

"A push, right. That's what we gave you and why everybody thought Gaylord Hospital was a good place for you to get the cognitive and physical therapy you needed."

The attack on me was so awful that the medical community responded in an extraordinary way. I know the effect of that response, and if it were up to me, the extraordinary would became routine. The furor, the attention, the immense effort lead me to grasp how blessed I am. Dr. Kurtz, Nurse Babb, and Dr. Cohen were some of the people who gave me hope, who fueled my will to recover. May others be equally fortunate, I think.

◆

Surgeons are notorious for being cold, unemotional. They pride themselves on "honesty," often delivering terrible news with as much inflection as a telephone operator and priding themselves less on interpersonal relationships then on their skill with a knife.

But Dr. Robert C. Della Rocca, an eye surgeon (for the past

twenty years chief of ophthalmic, plastic, reconstructive, and orbital surgery at the New York Eye and Ear Infirmary, and now also chairman of the Department of Ophthalmology at St. Luke's–Roosevelt Hospital and clinical professor of ophthalmology at New York Medical College), is my buddy. He's the man who saved my eye, and while I have no memory of the operation, I've seen him from time to time afterward, both as doctor-patient and as friends. His caring extends to many others. I know that he and his wife have established a foundation to work on the eyes of the underprivileged in Latin America, and that he has given himself tirelessly to the cause of health care around the world.

To get to his office, I have to walk through a waiting room jammed with eye patients, a sea of them, and I'm made conscious that my left eye, once askew in its socket, the muscles incapable of movement, can now swivel and focus as well or better than my right. From what Dr. Kurtz told me, what Dr. Della Rocca did was extraordinary; he was the best.

He's not in his office when I arrive, but he enters shortly thereafter, a stocky, white-haired man, apologizing for his lateness—he has just finished his third operation of the day (it is 3:15 P.M.) and is running behind schedule. He hugs me, then runs a hand over the scar beside my eye with the gentleness of a mother caressing her baby.

We sit facing one another. He tells me that Dr. Kurtz called him in for a consultation two weeks after the attack, but since I was still in such bad physical shape, he decided to postpone an operation rather than risk the further battering that surgery would require, despite enormous pressure from the press and second-guessing doctors who urged him to do it right away. By

May 17, though, I was strong enough, and Dr. Della Rocca, along with Dr. Craig Foster, a plastic surgeon, and other doctors, set to work.

Dr. Kurtz had told me that Dr. Della Rocca made an incision around the eye and teased the eyeball out of its trapped position, then resurfaced the floor of the orbit with a sliver of bone he took from the outer table of my skull to form a bone graft. He put that graft under my eyeball and moved it back up so it could be pulled back and forth, as it is supposed to be, by the muscles.

"I hate to use the phrase *cutting edge*," Dr. Della Rocca says, "but it was certainly surgery as updated as you're going to get. It's difficult when you work on the bones around the eye, repositioning the eye. You've got to support the eye so it takes off some of the pressure from the optic nerve. We had to not only stabilize the tissue around the eye, but you had some forehead bones that Craig Foster fixed, and I think there was a nasal fracture. It took around five hours. We had to go through the internal tissue, both through the mouth and also through the areas that tend to make a scar more obscure—underneath the eye, above the teeth, going in from the side a little bit so you limit the scarring. And then we put a little implant under your eye too, bone from the skull with metal on the rims."

"Was Jane Haher with you?" I ask, remembering the plastic surgeon who had worked on the scar a year later to make it less noticeable.

"Yes. A wonderful person. She was fully involved too." He sighs. "It was a charged atmosphere, charged even in the medical situation. What had happened to you took hold of the whole city, so you were surrounded by other doctors and the press—I had to fight my way out of the OR, I remember, because reporters came running after me. Metropolitan was almost like an armed camp."

He comes back to the present. "As you write your book, I think you're going to find out things in yourself that you think are pretty good. In the end you're going to say, 'You know, sometimes in life we're tested in certain ways. It's not fun to be tested.' "

"No, it's not," I say, in harmony with him, grateful to see his surgeon's manner melt away. "But a lot of good can come out of it."

"There are some things about it that only you can know, and you've dealt with that so well. That's what I see in your eyes." His stare is intense. "It's a strange thing. I dealt with my own emotions during that time—I have children who're now thirty-four, thirty-two, and thirty, and I felt a tremendous anger about the attack on you. It's not that when you take care of someone you don't have emotions. Of course you have them. You've got to keep them subdued, obviously, but there was no doubt in my mind that you came back from a very, very extraordinary medical-surgical situation, and that return allowed you to be what you are now, as a person, despite what you went through.

"I'm sure prayer has something to do with it," he continues. "I'm someone who believes in that. It helps you when you're a doctor and you don't think you're able to do something because you're just as fallible as everybody else, when you don't think you can reach a certain level that has to be reached." He pauses. "It's not so much prayer, it's spirituality."

He has put into simple words the enormous idea that governs my journey. "My wife is an unusual lady. She's involved with therapeutic touch, and she has a special way about her. Touch is in every area. Just before I operate on someone, I touch their face to feel what their face is about. You can feel their emotions a little bit, and your hands, somehow, maybe transfer a little bit of comfort at a time when people aren't feeling comfort. You have to help them take certain steps, the next phase of it, to whatever they have to encounter. All you do is help them along, that's all you do. I don't know what you experienced yourself, we didn't talk much about it, but I have to believe that it was of some help."

More than help. I have no idea what shape I would be in now if I hadn't experienced it. "I know there is a power there," I say.

We stand. He is looking at me with love, and again he touches my face. "You have beautiful eyes," he says. Recently, a New York City pretzel vendor—a stranger who knew nothing of what these eyes went through—told me the same thing, and I had thought of Dr. Della Rocca's work. Still, I start to protest his kind words. "No, you do," he insists, "you have beautiful eyes. They were probably beautiful before, but they sparkle more now. And I think that's a wonderful thing."

I come away thinking that Della Rocca is the gentlest doctor I've ever encountered. I always knew there was something special in him, a tender spirit, but when he started talking about the power of prayer and the power of touch—he had never before been so explicit—and when he touched my face one last time, I was left speechless. I just thought, "Wow."

◆

I know now that while I was comatose, great forces, both medical and spiritual, were working on my recovery. I don't understand precisely the power of connection—perhaps I'll never know. But amazing things happened in the darkness and led me back to this shining world. By the time I went to Gaylord Hospital for rehabilitation on June 7, I was able to play a far larger role in my own rehabilitation. True, I continued to get tremendous support from therapists, family, friends, and strangers, but more and more of this miraculous thing called recovery was now up to me.

Chapter Four

Gaylord

When memory returns after a traumatic brain injury (TBI), it arrives fitfully. Sometimes lightbulbs flash in the head the way they do in comic books; sometimes what is recalled is misty, jagged, as elusive as mercury. To retrieve my time at Gaylord, particularly the first weeks, means scouring my brain for details, which, even with all my concentration, I can't always unearth. Several people who treated me fourteen years ago still work at the hospital, so I've relied on *their* memory for aspects of my rehabilitation, yet their recollections sometimes conflict with my admittedly cloudy ones and leave me further confused. What's clear is that I arrived on a stretcher unable to work the buttons on my shirt, remember where I was supposed to go for my therapy sessions, or think on any but the most rudimentary level, and five months later walked out of the place prepared to face the world.

To do that meant *work:* days of the same physical and mental exercises, essential for establishing a routine for anyone with a brain injury; frequent frustrations, occasional setbacks, episodes of discouragement and despair.

To get through, I did not think of the past or the future, of where I had come from and where I would eventually wind up if and when progress stopped. Nor did I measure myself against the other patients. Rather, I concentrated on what I had to do— was instructed to do every day. Each sign of improvement, no matter how minuscule, spurred me forward. On Tuesday, say, I could manage to stand by myself; on Wednesday, take a step using the parallel bars; on Thursday, take two steps. There were more advances than failures, and I held on to them firmly, focusing on what I had achieved rather than on how insignificant the achievement was. I'm told I never complained. Of course not! I was too tired.

◆

Gaylord is a 109-bed, nonprofit rehabilitation center for adults. It was established in 1902 as a treatment center for tuberculosis patients—Eugene O'Neill was its most renowned "guest"— but in the 1950s, with the discovery of medicines that conquered the disease, it turned to other forms of rehabilitation: pulmonary disorders, strokes, spinal cord injuries, and brain traumas.

Its campus is set in the hills of Wallingford, Connecticut, flanked by a golf course and woodlands that take up much of its five hundred acres. Visiting now, I am impressed by its serenity; fourteen years ago, I found it big and intimidating and, with the numerous intersecting corridors of the hospital building, confusing. And my rehabilitation was anything *but* serene.

◆

My arrival, I've been told, was an event. Unbeknownst to me, many meetings had been held by administration and staff on how to handle "the Central Park Jogger" (treat her as you would any other patient, *but don't make any mistakes*) and the press (refer them to the hospital's public relations department, don't talk to them yourselves; *don't let them in the hospital building*). I came in an ambulance lying on a stretcher with my brother Bill at my side, the rest of my family and Pat Babb following in a car. What I remember most about the two-hour ride, which seemed to hit every bump between New York City and Wallingford, was thinking, "All I care about right now is getting through this ride without getting sick to my stomach." I didn't reflect on where I would be going, or what conditions would be like when I got there; I was just paying attention to the present, and the present was uncomfortable. I knew my family was beside me, that it would be okay as long as I didn't throw up in the ambulance.

I recall watching myself on the news being taken into Gaylord on a stretcher, but little else about that afternoon or evening.

In fact, for the first weeks, I was conscious of a heaviness in my head and body. When I moved, it felt as if I were pushing through mud. I wasn't in acute pain, exactly. Ironically, the only place that really hurt was my mouth, and this was not from the attack, but from my eye surgery. The only medication I can remember taking was Dilantin—not a painkiller, but used to prevent seizures.

Dr. Marilee Sipski, my attending physician, examined me almost immediately:

PHYSICAL EXAMINATION

The patient is a thin, White female in no acute distress. She is somewhat lethargic, found lying in bed, but is pleasant and cooperative and speaks in a hushed, pleasant tone. She is awake and oriented to person and place and grossly to time.

Head has recently been shaved for surgical repair with hair growth resuming. There are multiple well-healed scars over the left fronto-temporal and orbital region. She is wearing a moisture-retentive see-through left eye patch. There is complaint of diplopia at the extremes of upward and downward gaze. Lateral eye movements are grossly symmetric. Extra-ocular muscle movements are not grossly impaired. Acuity is reduced with a history of long-standing myopia. Pupils are equally round and reactive. Nose is patent. There are healing areas in the upper palate on the left side. Swallowing is intact for secretions but there is some incoordination of oral movement and a slight dysarthria. There is a mild left facial droop but it cannot be identified as an upper or lower motor neuron lesion due to the scarring. The tongue protrudes midline. . . .

. . . Speech is conversant with mild word-finding deficit. Content is somewhat superficial but she is able to converse

and follow the subject matter, although with some intermit-
tent confusion over not only recent but remote dates and
time. There is a peri-traumatic amnesia. Behavior is socially
appropriate and cooperative at all times.
   . . . Hand movements are characterized by mild incoordination. Static sitting balance is good, dynamic sitting balance fair, standing balance poor with ataxia noted. . . .
Anorexia nervosa by history.

PLAN:

The patient will be admitted to the Traumatic Brain injury program involving Physical, Occupational and Speech Therapy,
traumatic brain injury group to achieve a supervision/inde-
pendent level of functioning in mobility. . . . Cervical spine
films with flexion and extension views will be obtained to
evaluate the upper extremity paresthesia. An initial psychiatric evaluation will be obtained. Neurological follow-up will
be obtained as needed.

The next morning, the plan was put into effect. I was examined
by Lynn Luca, my physical therapist, in my second-floor room,
then taken down in a wheelchair to the physical therapy gym to
work with Lynn under the supervision of Nelson Carvalho, the
director of physical therapy. Speech therapy and occupational
therapy would commence the same day.

Nelson remembers me as "a tiny little thing, all huddled up
into your wheelchair, looking very sad and forlorn and sort of
pathetic. Your knees were up to your chest and you just looked
very frightened and were still pretty banged up. Not wearing the
flashiest of garb, shorts and a T-shirt and high, white socks."

Lynn remembers me pretty much the same way. As for me, being surrounded by mats, parallel bars, and other equipment, *and able to identify them*, gave me a good feeling. Other patients were in the room, some of them sitting, as I was, in wheelchairs against the wall, some lying on the mats or walking with the aid of the parallel bars.

I couldn't stand, at least not without assistance, and of course couldn't walk unaided, but, as Lynn later reminded me, I could roll over—I was, she says, a very good roller right from the start. She knew because this was the first exercise she had me do: lie on a mat and roll over.

My room was spare but comfortable. I had a private bathroom, just a sink and a toilet, and I believe there was a sink in my room as well—a sink and a mirror. When I gazed in that mirror for the first time, here's what I saw: I had a see-through patch on my left eye, which made me look like a miniature Long John Silver. The hair on the top of my head, where the surgery had been performed, had not yet grown in. The hair in back had not been touched, and with a hat covering the stubbled area on which the surgery scar ran across the crown of my head, I looked almost "normal." Most of the bruises on my body had faded, but both sides of my face and head had scars, raw from the beating and surgery. My family hadn't told me how bad the scars were. I can't remember what I felt when I saw them. Maybe I simply wasn't able to deal with the feelings. At least, I thought, I'm still here.

For the first days—it might have been as long as a few

weeks—I was wheeled to the various therapy rooms and to the showers. Soon, though, I could wheel myself, and each morning I looked at my daily schedule, a copy of which I carried with me, of where and when I was to go for my different therapies; each time I showed up at the right place at the right time was a mini-triumph.

Early on, a nurse handed me the week's menus—a sheet of paper with columns giving a choice of meals for each day. I, formerly anorexic, distinctly remember looking at it and thinking, "How unusual; I'm having to pick out entire meals. How do I feel about this? Do I want to do it?" The answer that came to me was "Yes, my body really needs this food. I haven't been good to it and I need to give it the nutrients it needs so I can get better."

I wanted to nourish my body, but like a baby I had to learn how. From the age of fifteen, I had lived mostly on small portions of salads and vegetables. Now I wanted more, but I didn't know what to eat. My psychologist at Gaylord, Dr. Susan Bookheimer, recently told me that initially I selected only salads and yogurt, despite my sense that I chose full meals from the menu—I even recall eating them. Whether I ate full meals or not, the good news was that my preoccupation with food centered on eating it, not "hiding" it the way I had done in the past.

My desire to starve myself had disappeared.

My college friend Ardith, who lived in Ridgefield, Connecticut, came to see me frequently; another dear friend, Jane O'Mahoney, from Chicago, had, luckily for me, decided to spend her summer in Connecticut and was able to visit often; Kevin O'Reilly was with me on several weekends; Steve and his wife, Leigh, were in Hartford and were always available. On Saturday, June 24, to celebrate my twenty-ninth birthday, they, along with Bill and his wife, Karen, and Ken and his girlfriend, came to see me. There is a group picture that shows us all dressed up, me with a new hat that covered the incision scar, like British aristocracy at a lawn party. It is difficult to tell from the picture that anyone is sick (my wheelchair was the only clue), or that we were at a hospital. Thinking about that day now, I realize that they can never know what it was like to be in my situation, but that I, in turn, will never know the worry, the pain, the empathy, and the suspense the attack inflicted on them. This was a momentous day, a graduation from patient to social being.

In the meantime, Lynn was teaching me how to walk. There were three half-hour physical therapy sessions a day, and I came to look forward to them. We used a roller-walker at first, the kind you see the elderly using, and soon I was able to travel seventy-five feet, walking unsteadily and having trouble with my balance and double vision—those never-ending exercises on the parallel bars also helped. We then gave up the walker, since Lynn was afraid I would grow too used to it, and I took to relying on her for support. She would walk with me down the corridor outside the physical therapy gym, and pretty much the way a child is taught to ride a two-wheeler bicycle, she would let go of me so I could take a few steps and later many steps on my own. Balance remained a problem, exacerbated by my having spent much of the last seven weeks lying down. Putting one foot in front of the other required enormous concentration.

As I used the wheelchair less and less, the exercises got more grueling. One of the problems was that I had to *think* about how to make my muscles move. Lynn had me walk to a point in the corridor, pick up an object from the floor, then walk back. I did heel-to-toe exercises, some on my hands and knees to strengthen coordination, and one called crisscross walking, requiring me to put one foot behind the other and move sideways. This last was tough; I fell a lot. By August, I was doing jumping jacks and "quick runs": start here, run to that line, come back. Lynn and a therapist named Diane would also strap me onto a tilt table, which, when raised, stretched my ankles, tightened by inactivity. It hurt like hell.

One day, I walked to the shower by myself! The shower was at the end of my corridor. When I first arrived at Gaylord, I had to be wheeled in by a nurse, who helped me off with my clothes and washed me while I sat in a chair. Sometime later, I would wheel myself and wash myself, still sitting, with a nurse supervising. That same nurse went with me after I could walk unassisted to the shower and wash myself; she was there to make sure I didn't fall. But now no nurse came with me, and I stood in the warm water, luxuriating, euphoric. (I relish showers even today.) A similar feeling, though not as intense, came over me when I was able to shave my legs, something you'd be unwise to attempt if your coordination was off.

And I remember with enormous pleasure the day when, after the patch was gone, I looked in the mirror and was able to put on mascara. To most women, it's an almost automatic act, but to me it meant a coordination of fine hand movement that just days before had seemed impossible. It also meant that I had reached a stage where some vanity had returned. To focus on how pretty my eyes looked—well, you can imagine.

I remember my therapists, the friends and colleagues who came to visit me, and a hundred incidents, but not the names or faces of any other patients. This was true even during a "high level" memory class, run by Dr. Bookheimer, where we practiced, among other things, learning the names of new people and remembering written material. I realized quickly that while I was able to do the exercises, others couldn't. I remember feeling empathy toward them and gratitude that I was progressing. Tired too. Exhausted. I had never taken naps, but needed them now, and by seven o'clock at night, all I wanted to do was sleep.

I had no idea of what level I'd reach, and though I certainly didn't believe I would be able to do everything I had done before I was attacked, I remembered thinking, "You know what? It's going to be all right." This realization didn't come in a flash. It alternated in my brain with dire questions like "Will I ever walk again?" or "Will I ever be able to function the way I did before?" There was no specific incident I can point to that convinced me I'd someday rejoin the world of my past. Rather, it was the accumulation of small victories, such as buttoning my shirt or remembering at lunch that I'd eaten cornflakes for breakfast. I remember the bursts of joy that accompanied each of them, wanted more of them, and so tried harder.

Two things made me believe I'd return to Salomon. First, Tom Strauss, its president, called me soon after I got to Gaylord and left his *home number.* Would he have done that if he didn't expect me back? And then my dad told me Salomon had a job waiting for me when I got out. This gave me a feeling of confidence and safety. "Did you get it in writing?" I joked.

With the realization that I would get better, though I didn't know how *much* better, I was able to achieve something that now seems miraculous: a sense that wherever I ended up, whatever I would be able to do, it would be enough. More than hospitals and therapies lay in my future. My physical improvement, increased ability in comprehension and cognitive skills, were further evidence.

Some moments made this feeling all the more important, for I experienced failure and fear as well.

Toward the end of June, Ardith brought me some books, and when she left, I picked the shortest one to read. (I wish I remembered the name; Ardith doesn't remember either.) But when I turned the page, *I couldn't recall what I'd read on the previous page!* The words and their meaning had vanished, as though a magician had played a cruel trick.

My terror then remains a visceral feeling today. I had done well in reading comprehension exercises in therapy, but now, not only could I not understand, I could make no sense of the book whatsoever.

I recognized my physical limitations from the start—it doesn't take genius to realize you can't walk. But my failure to remember what I'd read a second ago meant something was wrong in my mental and intellectual capacities. I was devastated. It brought me back to the time at Metropolitan when I couldn't draw two o'clock. I was embarrassed, ashamed, frantic about the future. No one will want to be with me, I thought. They'll see my deficiencies, realize how stupid I've become—I, who was always praised for my "smarts." I experienced moments of utter despair. My God, I can't even read a book!*

◆

There was also the matter of my slurred speech. And my memory for words was still shaky. I'd know that the red, roundish object Arlene Schwartz, my speech and cognitive therapist, showed me was a fruit, and even that it could be used in a pie. But *apple* was beyond me. (I still sometimes have trouble finding words. If I can't come up with the name for something, if someone gives me the first syllable or even the first letter, as Arlene did, usually I'll recover it.) I had trouble writing clearly; when asked to compose a paragraph on, say, my family, I'd wander off the topic.

Arlene gave me all sorts of exercises: making me imitate syllables, then words, then sentences; showing me pictures of objects I was supposed to name; having me make lists of items in a category, like meats and vegetables; teaching me tricks for mentally organizing my environment so I wouldn't forget where I put things (it helps today when I've mislaid, say, my car keys); reading me paragraphs and quizzing me on what she'd just read. She had me do exercise after exercise, which grew progressively more complex as the days went by, until she was joined by an

---

*I kept the book with me long after I left Gaylord, telling myself that I'd read it again but never doing so because I had the irrational fear that I would never be able to read it. During a move years later, I thought, "You know what? I don't want this book around anymore," and threw it away. Curious, isn't it, that I can't remember its name.

"academic therapist," Roni Keitel, who helped me with mathematics and reading, skills I would need when I went back to my job.

I took to the "mental" aspect of my rehabilitation just as I did to the physical and went through the exercises and tests with a drive Arlene found unusual. By focusing on going forward, I was mostly able to blot out thoughts of the distance I still had to travel. When by the end of June I was able to read a page and remember it when I turned to the next one, it was a huge step forward, not a reminder that any child of eight could have read it more easily. I concentrated on Arlene's exercises because I *could* do them; I needed the positive reinforcement and tried, not always successfully, to put out of my mind the existence of that incomprehensible book in my room.

◆

One disability I could not overcome revealed itself when I was still in a wheelchair. My occupational therapist, Mary Zack, and I were making cookies. I'm not a cook, though I had been a pretty good baker as a kid, and this kitchen activity wasn't too challenging. Nevertheless I worked at it diligently and so was pleased when Mary took the cookies out of the oven.

"I can't smell them," I said.

"You *can't?*"

"No," I realized with a shock. "I can't smell anything!"

She rushed to a cupboard, brought out two vials of what must have been obnoxiously odorous substances, and stuck them under my nose. "Well?" she asked. I shook my head.

My sense of smell did not return. The likeliest reason is that my olfactory nerves had been permanently damaged in the attack, though some people have lost the ability to smell without harm to those nerves. Friends, knowing that taste and smell are inextricably intertwined, ask me if it detracts from the enjoyment of eating. I tell them this: Until the attack, I got *no* pleasure from food, and now I don't know—*can't* know—what I'm missing. I appreciate food in a very real way, but when I read about gourmet meals or the smell of a freshly baked pie, I regret my loss. Still, I remember thinking at the time, if this was the worst aftereffect of the attack, I could get used to it.

It wasn't.

Mary guided me through other exercises as well. One was put-the-nail-in-the-hole. I was given a block of wood with drilled holes. Some of the holes were filled with nails, others were empty, and I was to use tweezers to transfer as many nails as possible from filled holes to empty ones within a given time. Obviously I was relearning manual dexterity. One day my mother was watching me. "I'd never have believed you'd be able to do that with such intensity," she told me. "It would drive me crazy."

How *else* would I do it? I did not consider it strange that I, an honors graduate from Wellesley and Yale, took such pride in moving nails around. Rather, I was showing off for my mom. "Look how far I've come," I was saying. That her twenty-nine-year-old daughter was still "in kindergarten" must have worried and terrified her, but I, of course, was incapable of such nuanced thinking at the time. I was a very young child in an adult body, learning to walk, learning to talk, learning not to drool, and learning the fine motor skills most adults take for granted.

◆

Sometimes we patients were taken by van to the nearest available pool for a kind of physical therapy I particularly enjoyed, although being transported in a wheelchair, as I was during the first weeks, was slow and arduous. The pool is perfect for exercising weak limbs, and for movement and balance; the support of the water takes away the fear of falling. Four or five of us would stand in a circle, moving our arms and legs, standing on one leg, moving forward and backward, bending our knees, basically changing our centers of gravity and increasing our strength. I had my own sensory issue, a feeling of heaviness in my legs (and to a lesser extent my arms), something that persists even today. The water helped, though the exercises were hard at first, as demanding as the exercises Lynn put me through.

I remember clearly finally being allowed to swim on my own (the therapists kept one of the pool's lanes open) and the pleasure that feeling of freedom brought me. I remember too a young intern named Eric. When I saw him approach, my balance in the pool suddenly became a lot worse and I would need him right beside me to make sure I was able to stand up. Our legs touched, and I experienced a shock of sexual attraction. Given that I was still pretty much bald, my head a mass of scars, my eye socket covered with a patch to prevent it from getting wet, and my face more Picasso than Renoir, I doubt the attraction was reciprocated.

◆

The triumphs grew more significant. On a Saturday afternoon at the beginning of July, Steve asked me if I wanted to go with Leigh, him, and my friend Jane to a movie. I wasn't feeling stir-crazy at Gaylord exactly, but I wanted to get "off campus." It was an everyday activity, yet a huge adventure, a test, and it brought me back into the real world. The movie was *Field of Dreams*. I still wasn't able to walk steadily—Steve had to help me to a seat—but the big news was that I not only stayed through the movie, but I *understood it:* "Build it and they will come." If you think this doesn't sound like much, imagine what it meant to a woman who just a few weeks before couldn't distinguish between the big hand and the little hand on a clock.

In late July, Jane and I attended a jazz concert on the New Haven Green. The two of us went alone, a milestone. Jane and I didn't discuss the possible perils of the trip beforehand—we just went. I have no idea now who the musicians were, but the concert was free and the green was crowded. To navigate my way through the people sitting randomly on the lawn was a big test. I missed my footing from time to time and sometimes had to hang on to Jane. But I felt ordinary, anonymous in the crowd. Ordinary was wonderful.

◆

On July 12, I had a visit from Elizabeth Lederer, the prosecutor assigned to my case. I had met her at Metropolitan, but now for the first time I would hear the details of the attack. Salomon had hired a lawyer for me, Mary Jo White, because the company wanted to make sure I had a legal advocate. Mary Jo sat in on the Gaylord session with Elizabeth but was later replaced by Larry Pedowitz when she took the job as chief assistant U.S. attorney in the Eastern District of New York.

What do I remember most about this key meeting? That I got

out of my wheelchair at the door of the conference room and walked without assistance, "standing tall," to greet Elizabeth! Even more than not wanting her to see a victim—perhaps too complex a thought for me—I wanted her to see how much I'd improved. What a difference from our meeting at Metropolitan, when I couldn't walk at all and can't remember what was said.

Elizabeth is a slight woman with curly brown hair and a stern professional manner that seems intimidating until she softens into a smile. At Metropolitan she visited me when I was just coming back to consciousness to ask me what I remembered about the attack. She needed to know what I knew before anyone else had a chance to tell me anything about it. The answer was nothing. I was still "fuzzy," and all I knew was that I had been hurt. She was gentle because I was so vulnerable and in a general way told me that she believed a group of kids had beaten and sexually assaulted me. I don't remember my reaction or her statement. I must have absorbed something about being raped, however, for soon after I asked Kevin how he felt about it. He said it made no difference to him.

Now, at Gaylord, she reported on the progress of the investigation, which was then still in its early phases. I found out that six had been indicted on charges related to the assault on me, and on charges relating to attacks on others as well. She asked me about my running routine and what I wore when I went jogging. Then it was my turn for questions. I asked her about the assault. Elizabeth told me about it, then read the charges in the indictment: riot, robbery, assault, sexual abuse, rape, sodomy, attempted murder.

Sodomy! I froze. This was new. I swallowed, winced, sat up straighter, the muscles in my buttocks involuntarily clenching, my breathing suddenly rapid. I imagined the violence, the pain. The words "attempted murder" passed by me, barely noticed.

Elizabeth remembers my reaction: "Did you have a nice trip? How was the traffic on the way up?" I asked her.

The denial and outward lack of emotion in my response now seems astounding. I knew I had been raped, yet because I had no memory of it, the impact on my psyche lacked the primal force that rape survivors describe so heartbreakingly. At that moment I couldn't handle this new fact—sodomy—so I mentally ran from it, blocked it out, though patently, according to Dr. Bookheimer, who attended the meeting, my body language spoke clearly of my internal reaction.

◆

When I discussed the meeting with Dr. Bookheimer later, she reports that I "was glad to learn the facts and began to express my anger at whoever did this to me." In her mind, I "had a better appreciation of the severity of the attack." I had already asked to speak with Barbara Moynihan, director of the Yale Rape Crisis Center.* After the meeting with Elizabeth, I reportedly began to "vent my anger" and became "more in touch" with my feelings about the assault.

Dr. Bookheimer quotes me as being shocked that anyone could be so depraved, but I don't remember how I responded. I know I didn't scream, break down, vow vengeance. I think that

---

*Barbara was called in early during my stay at Gaylord to educate the staff about how to work with a rape survivor in a coordinated way and to counsel them on dealing with their own reactions to the rape.

fury is what others expect, the "appropriate" reaction. But it wasn't mine.

Were my defenses so strong that I was able to compartmentalize what had happened so that rage didn't overwhelm me and prevent me from progressing in my rehabilitation? Was this the mechanism that let me cope with what might have been impossible to bear? Did my inability to remember blunt my feelings? Or was my lack of emotion the result of the injury to my brain? I may never understand just how or why my body and brain responded as they did. But I know they protected me, and for that I'm thankful.

Dr. Bookheimer felt the Gaylord staff was more upset by my case than I was. Several nurses requested psychological counseling to help them deal with what had happened to me, and others were so anxious to shield me from the outside world that they even kept back my mail, a practice that was stopped as soon as Dr. Bookheimer found out about it. There were some who were convinced that my positive attitude was a cover, a way of not facing up to what had happened, that sooner or later I would "break." They thought I needed to cry. It was difficult for me to be responsive to this type of psychological counseling.*

The question of whether I would testify against the accused was not brought up at the meeting. Dr. Bookheimer was afraid that, by testifying, I would "create a trauma that did not currently exist." My family felt the same way, I know. There would

---

*There was also understandable concern about exercise and my caloric intake. I was "penalized" if I lost weight by the denial of exercise privileges. Being "bribed" to maintain weight made me feel like a child. One therapist believed this attitude to be harsh and suggested that to beat the system I drink two glasses of water before getting weighed.

be later meetings about it with Elizabeth, who was eager for me to appear, not only for the sympathy I might evoke in the jury, but for another more vital reason as well.

◆

At one point—it was probably early August—Nelson Carvalho came up to me. "I have a group that gets together on Saturday mornings to run. Would you like to join us?"

"Run? Me?" I thought. It seemed I had just graduated from the wheelchair and had started to walk; running seemed too great a feat to attempt so soon. But soon enough, I said, "All right, I'll try."

I found out later that Nelson's suggestion wasn't impromptu, he had discussed it with Lynn, who agreed it was worth a go. There was a chapter of the Achilles Track Club based at Gaylord. (I am chairperson of their board of directors in New York City today.) Achilles is a worldwide organization that encourages people with all kinds of disabilities—amputation, arthritis, cancer, cerebral palsy, cystic fibrosis, multiple sclerosis, paraplegia, stroke, traumatic brain injury, visual impairment, and others—to participate in running. Nelson was the chapter's coach. The runners met on Saturday mornings, and I was excited to join them. No real competition was involved; it was just an organized way for people with disabilities to participate in running/walking, setting goals and achieving them. There were five or six runners in the club, and if they could do this with their disabilities, then so could I.

◆

The loop around the Gaylord parking lot, past the transitional house known as Traurig (short for The Louis D. Traurig Transitional Living Center), to the end of the driveway is approximately a quarter of a mile, the same length I had run with my brother Bill when I was in high school all those years ago. I found it incredibly long, full of small hills and dips that made running difficult. Nelson came with me, and when we approached the end, an uphill that looked as formidable as Mt. Everest, I was exhausted. He had to take my arm and help me across the finish line. To someone without a brain injury, those hills and dips are tiny blips on a flat track; I laugh now at seeing them. But then what I accomplished seemed monumental.

And, oh, it felt good! I was acutely aware that I was taking back something that belonged to me but had been taken away: the joy of running. It was different, because my legs were heavy, but I found that running—not the starting or stopping—was easier than walking; the momentum kept me going. We ran again the following weekends, and at some point I decided I could run on my own.

Nelson told me later that one of the volunteers who worked with the club kept a surreptitious eye on me, but I didn't know it then. When the makeshift quarter-mile track became too short for me, I ventured farther. At first I stayed on the grounds, running multiple times around the parking lot, but soon I began running off the hospital grounds, accompanied by Ed Amato, a hospital volunteer from town. This was difficult because it meant running downhill, my scariest challenge—it was hard for me to stop and still keep my balance. Once I mastered it, however, Ed and I would run a few miles outside the Gaylord "bubble." One day he didn't have time to run with me back to the hospital, so I ran alone and was spotted by a Gaylord employee, who reported me to hospital authorities. This caused a furor—I was unaware of how strict the hospital rule was that for my own safety and protection I was *never* to go out unattended.

The head injury: that really scared me. At Gaylord, I heard and saw the television and newspaper reports—*The woman who always tried to do everything in a superlative way, brain damaged!*—and I went into a panic that resurfaces from time to time even today. My God, to see myself so labeled by people I didn't even know, who had never seen or met me, was brutal. "Experts" would discuss the difficulties people with brain injuries would have in everyday life. They wondered how far I'd be able to come back, whether current disabilities were permanent, if I'd be able to function.

Imagine how awful it feels to a person with a brain injury to be called "damaged," no matter what the cause. It made we wonder—makes me wonder still—how people would react. Would they not take me seriously? Would they patronize me, treat me gingerly, hide truths and impressions in order not to upset me? Would genuine adult interaction be possible? I bristled when Nelson described me, sitting in a wheelchair, as "forlorn" and "pathetic" when I first came to Gaylord, true though it might have been. In fact, part of me still finds it hard to accept being called "the Central Park Jogger," for fear that people will only look for the damage and not see me.

It's this reason more than any other that I fought so hard at Metropolitan and Gaylord. I would *prove* I was capable of fully functioning, of becoming whole. Yet sometimes even now doubt creeps in if I can't remember a name or piece together past events or follow the intricacies of a spy-movie plot. These lapses may happen to everyone, but I feel they're more threatening to me. The aftereffects of the attack linger.

Chapter Five

"Thank You
for Your Prayers"

On the evening of April 21, 1989, a Friday, a man in his mid-fifties named Bob Herber was driving from Cambridge, Massachusetts, where he worked at the Institute for Foreign Policy Analysis, to his home in Marlton, New Jersey. He had just finished two hard days of editing and proofreading two monographs on international relations to meet the printer's deadline. The work had consumed his attention; he had not read a newspaper nor listened to a news report for forty-eight hours—as an expert on foreign affairs, this was unusual. Now he was looking forward to the weekend with his wife, Peggy. It was a chore to commute each week, but his job was in Boston and Peggy taught in New Jersey. Besides, he usually found the trip relaxing, and this time he could catch up on the news.

As he approached New York City, he tuned to WCBS, an all-news radio station, and found that one story so dominated the airwaves there was hardly room for anything else save traffic, weather, sports, and commercials. The story riveted him. A young woman had been savagely assaulted in Central Park and was barely alive. The police believed they had her assailants in custody. These teenagers had no earlier episodes of sociopathic behavior; there was no motive for the crime except violence. The teenagers used a word to describe it, *wilding*, which he had never heard before. Bob was furious.

"I almost didn't know where I was, listening to this," Bob said. "I just have this terrible hatred of violence against women. People do things like this to a woman, and I want to strike out. I'm a mild-mannered man, a devout Christian, but I had a strong feeling of revenge."

◆

I, of course, was the woman. Peggy had heard the stories about me for the past two days, and it was the Herbers' major subject of discussion all through Saturday. There was a guest minister at their Presbyterian church that Sunday, and the Herbers asked him if, during the service, he would offer a special prayer for me. The minister gladly obliged.

Bob became engrossed in the story. Before driving back to Cambridge on Monday, he bought the *Daily News*, the *Post*, and the *Times*, wanting as much information as he could get. There were, he realized, many similarities between him and the beaten woman, even though they were a generation apart.

I had been editor of my high school yearbook—Bob had been editor of *his*. I had applied for a Rhodes scholarship but had been turned down. He had the identical history. I liked exercise and the outdoors. So did he. The Herbers had no children of their own, but they had three goddaughters who were my age. And there was another link, perhaps the strongest of all. Bob's father had died on April 14, 1952, while Bob was in Europe on a Fulbright scholarship. Because he was traveling, he couldn't get home right away, so they held off the funeral until the nineteenth, April 19, the date I was attacked. The nineteenth, he knew, had more significance to him than the fourteenth; it was on the nineteenth he had felt the pain of his father's death—he felt a clear emotional connection to me.

Bob was not given to communicating his deepest feelings to strangers (nor was he a numerologist), but the coincidences were so strong that he felt a need to write to me, or rather to me and my parents, since I was comatose. On May 3, he sent a card decorated with flowers and a handwritten message for me:

> *We want you to know that you are always in our thoughts and prayers. We pray every day—many times a day—for your complete recovery, and will continue to do so until you are restored to health. And we know there are literally millions like us in America who are praying for you and your family. We only wish we could do more to help.*
> *But with God working through your doctors and nurses, with the love and support of your family and friends around you, and with your own spirit and fortitude and*

113

determination, we look forward to the day when we learn you have gone back to work and to running and to full enjoyment of life.

And a longer message to my parents:

> *My wife and I rejoice at the progress your daughter is making. We pray frequently, every day, every night for her complete recovery.*
>
> *. . . It is heartwarming that the outpouring of concern and love and admiration for your daughter extends across the country—as you must know. A few columnists are asking why the public and the media have devoted so much emotion and attention to her plight. I believe the answer lies not only in her ordeal and her heroic strength, but also and especially in her personal style, her brilliant academic record, her accomplishments in the workplace so early in life, her promise for the future, her industry and competitive spirit, her caring nature—and the many other outstanding facets of her personality as revealed in the profiles in the New York Times and other newspapers.*
>
> *. . . Any man and any woman would be proud to have her as a daughter. Hence, I believe, the great welling up of sympathy, love, hope, and prayers for the well-being of your daughter. . . .*

He received a form thank-you letter from Salomon on behalf of my parents; he had expected nothing more. But he kept himself informed of my progress. Bob told me that I continued to haunt him. We were, he was certain, attached.

He wrote to me on June 19, soon after I arrived at Gaylord, enclosing "a more tangible expression of our love and admiration for you": CDs of *Swan Lake, The Sleeping Beauty*, Handel's *Water Music*, jazz by George Gershwin and Claude Bolling, New Age music by Vangelis, and a tape he had made himself of excerpts from *Phantom of the Opera* and *Jesus Christ Superstar*. He didn't ask for an answer—just wanted to let me know that even though they were strangers, the Herbers cared about me, were sending their love and wanted me to heal.

Bob didn't want to seem intrusive or nosy, and he certainly didn't want me to think he was stalking me, so he didn't write often, but when he read in the *New York Post* that "SHE'S JOGGING AGAIN," he wrote on August 24, this time enclosing a vegetarian cookbook. "One didn't need a scorecard to know who 'SHE' is. I did a double-take, felt goose bumps swelling all over, and entered into a state of blissful euphoria."

"This was the first time I did anything like that," he said to me later. "I remember writing once, maybe twice, to widows of policemen who were alone with their children, and I'd made a contribution to that fund, but I never followed up on it. But this was a special thing. I wanted you to know that Peggy and I would do anything we could do to help you recover after you had finished in Gaylord."

◆

I *was* getting letters, dozens and dozens of them, even though it was well after a month since I'd been attacked. Those sent to me at Salomon were screened by Lisa Borowitz in the Corporate Communications Department, who then forwarded them to me at Gaylord. There are a few crazy people in the world and she wanted to make sure they didn't get to me. Some went to Gaylord directly. Pat Babb and my family had read the mail to me at Metropolitan; at Gaylord, I was shortly well enough to read the letters myself. I soon insisted that the staff not screen them—that I be allowed to open them myself. Some I answered personally, not many at the beginning, but most I sent back to Lisa for a response since I couldn't possibly answer them all. Among those I did answer personally were Bob's letters. His had such depth and passion. I could feel his love in them. I looked at them as if a normal person were writing to another normal person and there was nothing wrong with me.

Support from "strangers" was more immediately available at Gaylord as well. Either weekly or twice a month, a group of patients and their families met with former patients to talk about issues of living with a head injury. Steve and Leigh joined me in those meetings. What I remember most about them was the feeling of hope the former patients gave me. They still had problems, such as dealing with short-term-memory loss, slurred speech, or difficulty with walking, but they had been where I was now and they had progressed to where they were functioning successfully in the "real" world. Since I was unsure of how far my recovery would take me, their presence spoke of possibility.

As I've said, I'm not religious in the conventional sense. Still, there can be no question in my mind now that there is an intense connection between prayer and healing.

Scientific research supports my belief. I read Dr. Larry Dossey's book *Reinventing Medicine*, which reported on nearly 150 experiments on prayer and distant healing. I still get chills reading about the results. For example, in one study, conducted by cardiologist Randolf Byrd in 1982, 393 patients in the San Francisco General Hospital's Coronary Care Unit were randomly selected to either receive or not receive intercessory prayer. All participants—patients, doctors, and nurses—did not know which group was which. The patients who received prayer had less need of cardiopulmonary resuscitation (CPR), mechanical ventilators, diuretics, and antibiotics, and there were fewer occurrences of pulmonary edema, and even fewer deaths. In a more recent randomized double-blind study, conducted by Duke University and the Durham (North Carolina) Veteran Affairs Medical Centers, heart patients who were simultaneously prayed for by seven different religious groups around the world had better clinical outcomes than those receiving standard medical therapy alone. An Internet scan brought me to a double-blind study of advanced AIDS patients that found that when people prayed for them from afar, *without the AIDS victims knowing they were being prayed for*, they experienced significantly fewer AIDS-related illnesses, less severe illnesses, fewer and shorter hospitalizations, and improved mood.

At Metropolitan, when my life was at its most precarious, thousands of people prayed for me. Unknown to me, this was happening all over. At the Herbers' church; at the Church of the Heavenly Rest, where Salomon organized a prayer vigil; at a prayer group set up by neighbors of the alleged attackers; at services on Wall Street and in Harlem. And I survived. Did the prayers and the good wishes and the spiritual kinship of strangers create an actual *force* that surrounded me and helped me recover? I believe so.

As for the cards, letters, phone messages, presents: My family read and described them to me, even when I was comatose. Pat Babb, when she held me in her arms, whispered of the support and told me of the gifts from around the world sent to comfort me and help me get better. Did I subliminally understand their words and gain strength from that unconscious knowledge? I'm sure of it, just as I'm convinced that the cards and letters I *could* understand and read were a vital factor in the speed of my rehabilitation. No recovery was possible without the enormous skill of my doctors. But was there more? Did I have thousands of friends working on my behalf?

It was too early to ponder these questions at Gaylord; I was nowhere near capable of such abstract reasoning. The message was that I wasn't alone. I felt cosseted, comforted, not only by family, friends, and the staff but also by strangers.

I was hearing something else as well from the letters and cards: that I shouldn't be ashamed.

A common reaction among rape survivors is self-blame. "It's somehow my fault," the survivor imagines, and the internalization of that belief leads to shame, self-doubt, and silence. Some survivors feel they must hide that they were raped, so the attacks go unreported, while families and friends, in their own guilt or the desire to cause no additional harm, often fuel the shame by not talking about the attack with the survivor. Through this conscious denial they are in effect asking the survivor to deny the attack as well. Self-loathing takes the place of self-command, isolation replaces intimacy, and the survivor suffers quietly, often so profoundly that her life is destroyed. Our society is struggling to be more open about rape now, and books such as Nancy Venable Raine's *After Silence: Rape and My Journey Back* (1998) and Alice Sebold's *Lucky* (1999) have liberated other women to speak. But shame and secrecy are still all too prevalent, and the "my fault" syndrome has by no means disappeared.

Secrecy was impossible for me; the whole world knew I had been raped. But to me, this was a benefit. "*You* shouldn't feel ashamed," the messages were saying. "*We're* ashamed at how you were treated." People didn't ostracize me because I'd been raped. Rather, they opened their hearts to me. And, with few exceptions, I wasn't held responsible for the attack in Central Park.*

I wasn't alone, I was assured; my fight for recovery was a national fight. "I really don't know what to say, but I just want you to know I'm out here and I'm thinking about you" was a common way of reaching out to me, and the connection worked. Many wrote not to comfort me but to tell me how my recovery comforted them and gave them hope. "Your courage and strength really helped me."

A letter from a man named David Brody exemplifies the sentiments of 99 percent of the messages I received:

> *Dear Hero,*
>
> *You don't know me, and I hope that you don't mind my sending you this; but I really felt that I had to say this. . . . I just hope that you realize how deeply admired and respected*

---

*One letter came from a man who wrote me to ask "how dare you go into the park at night," but within a week sent me a note of apology.

you are, even by people you've never met, and never will meet. Actually, I doubt if you can realize it. How can you ever appreciate the strong feelings that so many people, even total strangers, have toward you! And I'm not talking merely about sympathy. Our feelings began as sympathy; but as we watched you make your incredible comeback, our feelings grew far beyond that. . . . What tremendous strength, courage, and determination you must possess! What a remarkable woman you must be!

And your example has produced practical results. You've given tremendous inspiration to so many others who needed it, and who overcame their difficulties with your unseen help. I'll tell you, truthfully, that I had some rough times myself this past year. Of course, they were nowhere near as rough as yours! But they were rough. However, watching you on the comeback trail gave me the inspiration that I needed to come through them, and to come through nicely. And I'm far from the only one. You've inspired so many people to weather their storms; and I mean good, worthy people—far more of them than you can ever know. . . .

Of course I realize that none of this can compensate you for what happened. (How can anything compensate you!) But I hope you realize that some good has come out of it; and I hope it makes a difference.

Imagine the power of all those words, all those messages! I feel uncomfortable reading such compliments now, but at the time, the support, acceptance, and praise was the air on which I floated. Early on at Gaylord, I may not have taken in the exact meanings in many of the letters and cards. But as I learned to walk, to speak, to master even the simplest processes of fending for myself, to *think*, I was able to internalize their cumulative effect and it bolstered my rehabilitation.

Support. Nothing could take its place.

◆

The variety of the support delighted me. There were poems, a handmade two-by-three-foot card from the elementary-school children and teachers of PS 27 in the Bronx saying, "I hope you get better." In Alaska, three hundred runners dedicated a 5K race to me and sent me a banner saying, "Hi Jogger—This Run's for You . . . May your recovery be as quick and brief as our arctic Prudhoe Bay Summers." A Boston woman, who writes me still, sent mass cards and calendars. I got hand-painted holiday cards from a man in Montreal that continued for years. And the great long-distance runner Joan Benoit Samuelson sent me a pair of running shoes, which I wore when I returned to the sport at Gaylord and ran that tentative quarter mile and have still, though they're worn thin and unusable. The 1989 Heart Association–sponsored 5K Wall Street Run was staged in my honor, and I wrote a message of thanks that was read before the race began. I wish I could be there running with you, I said, but I'm running here at the same time and will try to do the same distance.

A man sent me via FedEx a medal he had received upon finishing the New York City Marathon on November 5, 1989, just days before I left the hospital. He hadn't run a marathon for six years, he wrote me, but was inspired now to do so to honor me, and "so that you could have this medal as you came closer to finishing your own marathon." I was immensely moved that he would give this medal to a stranger. To me, the medal represented the training and work needed for such a run, and the experience of the marathon itself. I had never received a medal in any of the marathons I'd run, because I'd run unofficially and was never registered. His gift made me push harder. The man was from White Plains, New York, and I could easily have contacted him, even gone to see him. But it felt wrong. Our connection was the medal, an unspoken bond between us, and the medal still hangs in my bedroom.

And then there was Milli Wegner, a fiftyish woman from Escondido, California. I got a card from her at Gaylord, beautifully painted and expressing her sympathy. Then, the next week, another card, then another—a series of cards, which arrived regularly for years, containing copies of inspirational poems and simple thoughts. She sent letters of loyalty and concern too, notes that encouraged peace, love, and appreciation of nature. Her letters were often chatty—about her everyday life, what the kids on her street were up to, how she'd go to jazz concerts supporting local musicians. She sent me a tape of a singer I'd never heard of, a woman named Enya, and I loved the music and played it often. Having read of my love of the outdoors, she wrote of hers and told me of the closeness she felt between us.

Her letters continued for years—once every two weeks and later one a month; we were pen pals!—accompanied by presents on Christmas and my birthday: Waterford crystal, a ceramic bird, wood sculptures of animals from the San Diego Wild Animal Park, and some Native American horsehair pottery. Milli sent me beautiful books too, including a volume of reproductions of Georgia O'Keeffe paintings.

I reciprocated Milli's feeling of connectedness—her spiritual approach to life appealed to me—and while I hadn't given my name to the gentleman who sent me the medal, in her case I decided to reveal it—it felt funny to sign my letters "The Central Park Jogger" since we wrote so frequently.

She gave me her phone number, asking me to call if I felt like it. "Please call collect for two reasons," she wrote, "a) I may be at a complete loss for words in my excitement and b) I may never stop talking in my joy to hear your voice."

I did end up calling her, though never collect, and our long-distance friendship continued for twelve years. She was so regular in her writing that, last year, when more than a month had passed and I hadn't heard from her, I was afraid something had happened. I called many times over the next several weeks but never got an answer—she lived alone and did not have an answering machine. Then one day, a man answered the phone, her brother, and told me Milli had died of a cancer that had taken over her body in two months.

It was a great loss, like losing a family member. I told her brother, who didn't know me, how much she meant to me. "Here's a woman I loved and who loved me," I thought, "but we've never hugged. We had never looked in each other's eyes. And yet we'd touched each other so deeply."

◆

The Herbers also became like family. Bob's letters continued, warm and revealing. I got one on November 13, shortly after I left Gaylord, enclosing $100 as a Thanksgiving present for my recovery, with the instruction to "do something in the Big

Apple." I used it to buy tickets for *Les Misérables*. Another, dated April 11, 1990—fifteen pages long!—expressed his outrage at my having to appear at the forthcoming trial, and his fury at articles in *Time* and *Newsweek* that suggested I had been anonymous long enough. The issue meant a great deal to him:

> *Ms. Overholser, editor of the Des Moines Register,*
> *undoubtedly well-intentioned, is dead wrong in arguing*
> *(NY Times, March 25) that the press, by failing to identify*
> *the victim by name, does more than protect their privacy; it*
> *also compounds their stigma. RUBBISH! What stigma?! In*
> *what century is she living, or with what types of people does*
> *she associate? Among decent people, the stigma is not the*
> *victim's; it attaches solely to the rapist. If Ms. O. disagrees,*
> *then the solution for her should be educating the public, not*
> *publicizing the name of the victim. . . . Your triumph over a*
> *monstrous and tragic assault has, in every respect, exalted*
> *you as a young woman. I can't imagine any decent human*
> *being thinking otherwise. . . .*
>
> *In any event, no doubt you aren't the least bit interested*
> *in being an exalted person! What you want most of all*
> *now—next to complete recovery—is your privacy, a chance to*
> *get on with your life without further fanfare.*

The letter talked about the brave fight Bob's mother put up against bleeding ulcers (a victorious fight, when she was given a 10 percent chance of survival), which was something out of the ordinary for him; he rarely talked about his own struggles, only mine. Each time he wrote, of course, I wrote back, thanking the Herbers for their thoughts and their presents. The letters showed a level of loyalty and love I found unprecedented. These were good people, I felt. I could trust them.

In July, at the time of the trials, Bob and Peggy invited me to come to their house in New Jersey if I needed "some R&R." They had thought long and hard about asking me, Bob wrote, because they didn't want to intrude on my privacy. Nevertheless, they thought that they'd regret it if they didn't follow through on their instincts—there'd be no hard feelings if I turned them down.

I wrote them back on August 15. Yes! I'd like to visit them, I said, though not immediately since I was stressed by the tension of the upcoming second trial:

> *I was thinking while reading, before I reached your invitation, that it is silly that you know me only as "the Central Park Jogger." I realize it is only a name, as my real name is, but telling you my name signifies that I would like our relationship to be on a more personal level as I have come to trust and respect you. One reason "my anonymity" has been as important as it has been is not because I am embarrassed about or in any way, shape or form blame myself for being in the Park when I was, but rather to prevent the media from encroaching upon my life and making me a celebrity for a reason over which I have no control. In any event, I want you to know me and not some mystery person.*

I signed the letter "Trisha Meili" and gave them my home address. Bob read it while unlocking his car's trunk and was so surprised he nearly fell in.

In his reply, Bob told me he was overjoyed that I felt comfortable enough to want to meet them and to tell them my name. There was, I felt, a depth of trust between us I experienced with no one else save my family and dearest friends. And he wrote that after the first trial the accounts in the *New York Times* had made him feel I had gotten through it with grace and self-possession. Now that the worst was over, he continued, the Herbers were still concerned about me and would continue to stay in touch to give me whatever support I needed.

Reading Bob's letters now still moves me. He stands for all the people who lent part of themselves to me, who were my valiant army in the fight for that most valuable of all prizes: life.

I went to visit the Herbers in early November of 1991, and I've seen them many times since. Once, at a special occasion, when Bob read a passage from Kahlil Gibran's *The Prophet* about the importance of love, I knew there was no one better qualified.

◆

I received the comfort of thousands of others; I experienced an outpouring of support only a few of us are privileged to receive, but it wasn't me, Trisha Meili, who was being singled out. I'd become a symbol of something far greater than myself, and to repay all those who wrote or called or painted or prayed or wished or hoped for me and my recovery makes me happy.

There's more in my heart than I can possibly express, but this I *can* say:

Thank you for your prayers.

Chapter Six

Prepare for Departure

The Louis D. Traurig Transitional Living Center is located on the Gaylord grounds and visible from many of the hospital windows. Some with "acquired brain injuries" (Gaylord's term; it includes traumatic brain injuries like mine) reside there after they've recovered to the point they don't need the full-time, one-on-one supervision they receive as an inpatient in the hospital. They are medically stable and can get around by themselves (even if it's in a wheelchair or with a walker), as they will in the outside world—into which, as the word *transitional* implies, they will soon enter. Traurig's goal is to help brain-injured patients regain the basic skills of independent living and to restore them to the highest level of achievement possible. The availability of such a transitional living center was an important factor in my family's decision to send me to Gaylord.

I arrived at Traurig, a journey of some one hundred yards from my hospital room, on August 8. My mood was jubilant. I was now an outpatient! True, I was still on the Gaylord grounds, relearning almost everything that had once been second nature to me, but Traurig represented more freedom, and the staff was convinced I was ready for it. I would still work with all of the therapists who had helped me at the hospital, still need occupational therapy, speech and cognition therapy, physical therapy, and psychotherapy, but I was now in "graduate school." When I could show that I had recovered enough to take care of myself on my own—then I would be allowed to go home.

Traurig had room for twelve patients, though there were only eight of us when I got there. I was assigned a second-floor room since I wasn't in a wheelchair and, with considerable difficulty, could navigate the stairs. It was a pleasant and airy space. A man lived in the room next to mine; all the other patients were in wheelchairs and thus stationed downstairs.

I still had—the dreaded D-word—deficits. Perhaps most serious of all, my "executive functions"—attention span, concentration, decision-making abilities, responding to new or stressful situations, skills that were vital if I was to return to my job at Salomon—were impaired. These functions, located in the most highly developed part of the brain, are generally the last to return after an injury, since the wiring required for these skills is more complicated. In my brain, that wiring had been damaged. With therapy, some areas would heal, others would be compensated for by undamaged areas, and perhaps others would be permanently affected.

Even the day-to-day activities that are second nature to most people posed a problem at Traurig. I had to concentrate on routine things before I did them and so was acutely conscious of walking in a straight line, standing without losing my balance, planning a meal, and choosing what to wear.

Arlene and Roni worked with me to improve my cognitive abilities. They taught me to think things through sequentially, to be more aware of how long it might take to complete a task, to spot errors and correct them on my own. By this time, I was reconciled to the fact that I needed assistance. I was not in complete control of my physical functions or my thoughts, hence not the determined, stubborn, "go it alone" woman I considered myself to be before the attack. As a person who once saw asking for help as a sign of weakness, I had to come to terms with being dependent on others.

I worked practically nonstop. Roni's Academic Therapy Progress Report dated October 13 notes that at Traurig I had attended thirty-five one-hour group sessions of academic therapy and fourteen one-hour individual academic sessions, bringing me up to "college level in the areas of reading comprehension, vocabulary, written expression, mathematic number operations (addition, subtraction, multiplication, division, fractions, decimals, percentages), and mathematic problem solving." Add to this daily physical therapy, biweekly psychotherapy, and weekly group meetings with assault survivors.

No wonder I was exhausted by nightfall.

◆

During my time at Traurig, my psychotherapy continued with several therapists. I even saw a psychotherapist for my eating disorder. I don't remember much about these sessions, but I do recall feeling closer to some therapists than others. As best I can tell now, my psychological strategy, simply to deal with my present tasks, was an unconscious form of denial. I acknowledged intellectually that I had been beaten and raped, but denied the full extent of the trauma and instead focused on how I could overcome my deficits.

Others worried that this was not a healthy response. Dr. Bookheimer left in late August. In her notes, she wrote that I "had not experienced a profound psychological reaction at this time [my discharge from hospital to Traurig] and appears to have a deficit in the experience of emotions. Therefore, she is at risk for post-traumatic stress reactions and will remain so for a long time."

Dr. Bookheimer and others felt that I hadn't grasped the extent and implications of my difficulties. True, in June I complained to her of several cognitive problems, including short-term-memory loss, amnesia, word-retrieval impairment, as well as difficulty walking and double vision. But then and now I never saw or felt—never internalized—how close I had come to death or severe mental and physical disability. Does this speak to a "deficit in the experience of emotions"? I don't know. Some of my psychotherapists wrote that I was becoming more emotional, more "feeling," as I neared the end of my stay at Traurig, but continued to worry about the emergence of traumatic symptoms, such as nightmares and difficulty concentrating, later on. This was a particular issue in deciding whether I should testify at the trials.

Before the attack, I was easily influenced by others and tended to think that the last person I spoke with had the most convincing view. This got worse post–April 19, especially with some important decisions about my care, such as when I would leave Metropolitan and where I would go for rehabilitation. I needed help making them. I'm impressionable but stubborn. When I feel strongly about something, I can be fierce on my own behalf. At Gaylord, one of the marks of my cognitive improvement was that I decided for myself that I no longer needed Pat Babb's assistance (she left after my birthday party); I decided from whom and just how much I wanted to hear about the details of my assault. I decided it was time to see Elizabeth Lederer, not the other way around. And at Traurig, I planned where and for how long I'd run, and where I'd go and whom I'd see on my weekends "off campus."

◆

In the second week of September, Salomon arranged to set up a small cubicle in my room for use as an office. It took up half the space. Complete with a desk, filing cabinet, computer, printer, telephone, and Quotron (a computer monitor that tracked both the equity and fixed-income markets), it gave me a sense that I was back at work. Roni helped me relearn the machines and the mechanics. She refreshed me on use of the HP 12C calculator, algebra, stock market transactions, and flow charts. Salomon even supplied a small sign with the company's logo reading CONNECTICUT BRANCH attached with Velcro to the cubicle panel.

I had been doing small tasks for Salomon under Roni's direc-

tion, and on September 14, I got this piece of interoffice corre-
spondence:

TO: Trisha E. Meili   cc: Douglas T. Lake
                                 Merrick G. Andlinger
FROM: Peter Vermylen
RE: "The Company"

Trisha,
    Attached is a description of a project that Rick
Andlinger and I would like you to work on in support
of our new business efforts on the chemicals side of
The Company.
    Your past work on The Company may have exposed
you to their chemicals business to some extent, but we
now want to concentrate on it in greater detail, looking
for strategic business opportunities. . . .
    The Company study is something that Rick and I
have been talking about doing for some time, but until
now we have not been able to get going on it. With your
help we hope to get the ball rolling and add a profitable
new dimension to the Firm's relationship with The
Company. Both of us would be happy to discuss the
project with you at any time.
    I'll look forward to talking with you about it.

The attachment was headed "Energy and Chemicals Group"—
my group—and as its primary objectives it asked, among other
things, for a "solid understanding of The Company's current lines
of business," an analysis of The Company's current strengths and

weaknesses, and at least five good acquisition ideas to bring to The Company's attention.

Quite a challenge for a brain-injured associate.

I was eager to start working on an actual major assignment rather than the short tasks and the calculator and computer exercises Roni reviewed with me, but could I do it? It was daunting, relearning how to organize, prioritize, and find information in an actual business situation. I had to check and recheck my work. I consulted colleagues, trade journals, and news stories about The Company, working a few hours a day and feeling throughout that I had to show my bosses at Salomon I was okay and ready to get back to work.

At 1:30 P.M., October 6, I faxed my analysis to Peter. Without the brain injury, I would probably have finished it a week or two more quickly. I described the basic makeup of The Company, its history of growth through previous acquisitions, my view of its overall business strategy, and gave a breakdown of its annual sales and revenues in its various departments covering the years 1984 to—its strongest—1988.

The ball, I felt, had started to roll. It was up to Peter and Rick as to how to use the invaluable information I had provided.

At the time, it seemed to me that I was at last making a significant contribution to my company. This was serious stuff, I felt, information that Peter and Rick Andlinger needed. I believed I had researched it well and provided the information just as I would have had I been stationed in my New York office.

It didn't occur to me until much later that what I was doing might have been make-work, that Peter and Rick were being kind to me, as well as prepping me for the type of work I would actually be doing once I returned to Salomon. Had I thought it through rationally, I would have realized that no executive would have depended on a recently brain-injured employee to provide so important an analysis "for real." At the very least, they'd have had someone else check over both the figures I supplied and my analysis of them.

When, years later, I asked Peter's boss, Doug Lake, if they had indeed provided me with work simply to help me in my recovery, he said, "Of course," and when I asked him specifically about the report I had provided, he had no memory of it. "At this point you had a hard time concentrating," he told me. "And you had a hard time with your vision. Our aim was to provide you access to some work to sort of try to bring you back, develop some continuity in your life." And Roni told me that even before I left Gaylord for Traurig, she spoke with Pat Garrett and Terry Connelly so she could better understand what I did at Salomon and thus gain insight into how she could best help me. When I got to Traurig, she went to Salomon to see Terry and Doug Lake—it's probable that the idea of the "assignment" was born then.

But it sure didn't feel like make-work at the time. I approached it with all seriousness, and when I finished, I thought, "Wow, this is pretty good. It's a nice little summary."

In other words, the ruse worked. The knowledge that I could indeed respond to a project the way I had before the attack instilled confidence, enthusiasm, and a sense of worthiness— exactly as Peter, Doug, Terry, and Rick had intended.

◆

Meanwhile, I went on with other aspects of my therapy, both physical and cognitive. I saw friends and family on weekends—a movie with Steve and Leigh, a trip to Ardith's condo, visits with colleagues from Salomon, a local softball game. Gaylord found a woman who taught me basic ballet moves at the bar (we used a parallel bar in the Gaylord gym)—the trip to buy ballet shoes, tights, and a leotard was part of the therapy too. Once during the last month of my stay at Traurig, I took a self-defense course sponsored by the Yale Rape Crisis Center. Not that I could have defended myself against a serious attack in my current condition. The lesson was for possible later use. And I went driving.

To me, relearning to drive was a significant sign of independence, even though I rarely drove in New York City. Driving demands precisely the faculties I was deficient in: depth perception, reaction time for accelerator and brake, quick decision-making, and the ability to anticipate the moves of other drivers. I started lessons in October, using a computer-simulated model to test my response rate. Then, with a handicapped-driver trainer from the DMV at my side, I began driving off Gaylord's property. This meant negotiating the Merritt Parkway, tough enough considering the speeding traffic, and going through an eighth-of-a-mile tunnel, a feat that at the time seemed fraught with danger. I remember sucking in my stomach when we approached the entrance, to make sure the car would fit in the lane, and that small stretch of road still makes me nervous fourteen years later. In all, I had six and three-quarter hours of on-the-road evaluation. The instructor recommended that I not try independent driving without further work, so in New York City, when I was released, I stuck to letting others drive—or rode the subway.

Most important of all, during my stay at Traurig, I was allowed to go out of the hospital by myself for the weekend, on a "TV," hospital-speak for Trial Visit. That first weekend away I spent with Kevin.

❖

I was told Kevin had come to visit me virtually every day at Metropolitan (one of my first memories of those days was seeing him there), and he came to Gaylord on several weekends, much to my pleasure. I don't remember whose idea it was that I should visit him at his home in Montclair, New Jersey—his, probably—but we both embraced it, I as much for the experience of traveling alone as in the prospect of seeing him. I got permission to leave from Dr. Bookheimer.

How exciting it was to travel by myself! Though someone at Gaylord probably helped me with the logistics, it was still an intricate series of steps. First I had to get the schedule and figure out which train to take to Montclair, no meager achievement. Next, I had to call a cab to take me to the station. Then I had to climb up the train stairs, find a seat, and sit down, all without falling. Having covered my stubbly hair with a hat, I probably looked normal, but no one sat next to me and the trip was uneventful. Kevin was waiting for me at the station, and his smile and hug of greeting confirmed my delight in my accomplishment.

It was a quiet weekend. Kevin and I explored his neighborhood, me supported by his arm, which made walking much easier. It was a beautiful summer's day. I remember particularly the look of the green trees and grass and my gratitude that I was able to appreciate them. I remember also my sense of freedom, a feeling of euphoria that began from the moment Kevin met me at the train. I knew I could relax, that I didn't have to watch every step, monitor every movement, because he would take care of me.

That night, Kevin and I made love.

◆

A common reaction in surviving sexual assault is to shy away from sex, often involuntarily and often for a long time. Rape is such a violation, so visceral an act, that it poisons the body's sense memory. Much as the survivor might love the person she's making love with, physical intimacy is difficult. The act can trigger flashbacks or the general sense of being forced or coerced, with its accompanying feelings of loss of control and rage.

I recently read Dr. Judith Lewis Herman's book *Trauma and Recovery*, in which she notes that "if a survivor is lucky enough to have a supportive family, lovers, or friends, their care and protection can have a strong healing influence" (a study of rape survivors reported that the length of time required for recovery was related to the quality of the person's intimate relationships). But even in these cases time and tact are necessary, and the process can be slow.

Before my own reinitiation into sex, I'd wondered if having sex after my experience would be emotionally difficult for me. I even discussed it with Dr. Bookheimer. I didn't think it would be too traumatic, since I had no memory of the brutality of the attack, no horrible, painful feelings of powerlessness associated with the act of intercourse. Still, I wanted and needed to make sure. My fear was not related to my safety or to having flashbacks, but rather to *his* comfort: whether Kevin or any other man would want to make love to this "damaged property." I'd had tender moments with Kevin at Gaylord that made me feel comfortable about taking the next step, but still, it seemed to me precarious. I believe I started our lovemaking. Kevin would have been far too considerate not to wait until I'd signaled it was okay.

He told me later that he didn't have the sense that I had any sexual issues related to the rape. But he realized how important it was for me to feel that I was attractive in spite of what had happened. My vanity was obviously intact, he said, and he knew that making love would confirm it. His major concern was in being gentle, since I was frail and he didn't want to hurt me. I, as usual, didn't allow myself to think that I was frail—what I remember was feeling safe in his arms.

◆

Two weeks later I visited him again. On Saturday, Kevin invited some people from Salomon to join us. How normal it seemed. My friends treated me not as a kind of walking miracle—an attitude I was desperate to avoid—but simply as a colleague with whom they had been reunited. It was a pleasure to talk shop rather than recovery. The atmosphere was casual, warm, welcoming. I felt once again fully functional, "one of the guys."

Two weekends after that, I decided to visit New York. My therapist had encouraged me to go back to my apartment, since I was considering returning there after my discharge from Traurig. She suggested I not spend the entire weekend alone, but rather be with friends as much as possible. It turned out to be one of the most memorable weekends of my life.

◆

For weeks, I had wanted to see my apartment, *feel* my apartment and what it was like to be home. Tim Moore, whom the building's tenants had designated as their representative to my family when I was at Metropolitan, had visited me a few times at Gaylord; it was he who had watered my plants and taken care of my mail while I was away. Now he met me at the train and took me to the building in a taxi. "Oh, man, when I saw you, you were teetering on the stairs," he told me later. "You looked so weak." Again, I didn't feel weak—a little tired, perhaps, but delighted to be going home.

At Gaylord, I had often pictured my apartment, asking myself, "Okay, what do I remember?" It was a test I had devised for myself to see if I indeed had the memory problems I had been told might be an aftereffect of the attack, and now here I was at last to see for myself. I opened the door.

A table with all my plants on it was in the front hallway. That was new. Tim must have set it up to make watering the plants easier. Otherwise, the apartment was exactly as I'd pictured it. My favorite things—an Oriental rug I had bought on a trip to Chicago while visiting Jane; the stereo system I was supposed to show Pat the night of the attack; wood carvings I had brought back from Africa—enchanted my eyes, and I lay down on my bed in bliss. Yes, I'd have to go back to Gaylord. But sooner or later I would be here again. Permanently. Almost the same person who had lived in this apartment before.

That evening Kevin would pick me up, we'd have dinner out, maybe go to a movie, the familiar routine. Yes, that was it: familiar. It felt fabulous.

◆

My brother Steve had a good friend named Janet whose own brother was a priest. When I was at Metropolitan, he often came to bless me, always introducing himself with "Hi, I'm Bill, Janet's brother." Like everyone else, he was following Dr. Cohen's instructions that all visitors should identify themselves by name, even when I was comatose, to help with my orientation. After I left Metropolitan, on the few occasions I saw him, he'd introduce himself again: "Hi, I'm Bill, Janet's brother." It became a family joke. By this time, I *knew* who he was.

Father Bill was a runner. So before I came to New York that weekend I asked him if he'd run with me on that Sunday morning. It was September 10. By that time, I could run a little— slowly, awkwardly, but at a steady pace; the only real problem was stopping at red lights. We decided to go to Central Park, where there were no street crossings—yes, and then to run along the 102nd Street crossdrive, past the point where I was grabbed and dragged down the ravine to the eventual site of the rape.

It must have been my idea, since it's unlikely Bill would have suggested it. I had run there many times before the attack, but now it would be with a different awareness. I didn't think it would bring up bad memories because I had no memories, but I needed the reassurance.

Still, I certainly didn't want to go to that place alone. So this priest, this man I was comfortable with and could trust, was the ideal companion. I went to his church on the Upper East Side to pick him up, and off we went. Though my family had told me there was a memorial to me at the site, I could not have dreamed of its power.

◆

The memorial was a small ring of stones surrounding a variety of carefully arranged cut flowers—yellow, white, red, a true bouquet. Someone had planted marigolds. A small stick in the center bore an American flag, another was decorated with a large red bow. Other sticks carried messages. "Our Hearts Are With You," read one, handwritten beneath a painting of trees in winter and signed "Eddie V." "TO THE FALLEN RUNNER, PLEASE RUN THROUGH IT," read another, signed by the Sunshine Running Team of Clearwater, Florida. A professionally printed card read, "In this time of sadness many thoughts are there with you, for many people share your sorrow. So may these words of sympathy give you comfort now and help you find new strength for each tomorrow." One stick held a crudely hand-printed message addressed "To you, the unfortunate victim of this brutal crime." It went on, "We do hereby promise: We will continue to jog, walk and enjoy all of Central Park in even larger numbers and at any time, as is our right. We will use all the streets of New York unafraid . . ." There was even a note, on an official Parks Department form, placed on the ground and addressed "To Our Fallen Jogger" and signed by Eddie and Frank, Parks Department workers. "We know you are on your way to recovery," it read. "Keep up the good work."

People were still putting down fresh flowers and messages in September, five months after the attack! No one approached the memorial while I was there, and Father Bill stood tactfully off to the side as I gazed at it. I wanted to shout out, "I'm here because of your thoughts and prayers!" But instead I stood quietly and let that power, all those strangers' love, fill me. We had only run a little more than a mile to the memorial, but there would be no more running that day. I could not stop the tears.

◆

On Monday, September 18, I went to see Doug Lake, head of the Energy and Chemicals Group, "my" division at Salomon, to talk about my future. He had been on vacation in Rome at the time of the attack and had rushed back, coming to visit me at Metropolitan before he even went home. "You were beaten to a pulp," he remembered. "Your head was as big as a basketball."

We met at the lounge of the Westbury Hotel on the Upper East Side. Doug had blown out his knee in a tennis tournament, so he was on crutches, while I was carrying the cane I sometimes used to be sure of my footing. "You had huge balance problems," he told me later. "So did I." He stressed how anxious Salomon was to keep me; the issue was where I would work. Salomon had offices all over the world. Even though the New York office would honor my anonymity if I stayed there, my progress might be slowed by the distraction of the barrage of publicity that was certain to follow me anywhere I went. Dallas was an option, or San Francisco or Chicago. My own feeling was that I simply wanted to get back to what I was doing before the assault. I hadn't thought of leaving New York. Now I asked Doug for some time to think it over.

After several conversations with family and therapists to weigh the options, I still felt I wanted to return to the city. I called my father to discuss it. For some reason my mother wasn't on the line—our conversations were usually three-way—and what I remember gratefully was that he didn't start by saying,

"Here's what I think," but rather his message was that it was my decision. Like Doug Lake, my brothers, concerned about my safety, didn't believe New York was the right place for me. My parents weren't so sure either and were concerned about the negative effects on my recovery from the continuous media coverage. Everyone was worried that there might be retaliation from the alleged attackers' supporters, particularly since the trials were sure to start within a year. Yet after we had gone over the alternatives, my father simply said, "Well, what do you want to do?"

My inclination was to stay in New York.

Perhaps some of this was naïveté. I was still completely protected at Gaylord and Traurig and had little idea of the potential dangers lurking in a free environment. It was an instance in which my lack of memory kept me from the visceral fear of another attack. Then there was sheer orneriness. "Damn it," I thought, "no one's going to stop me. I'm not going to submit to letting anyone prevent me from doing what it is I want to do."

But mostly I wanted to stay because of the *comfort* of it. New York had become my home, and I had worked hard to get here. In Salomon's New York office, I would be surrounded by people I knew and who knew me. In a major way they had been partners in my recovery, had a deep understanding about what I had gone through and was going through now. True, I might be at less physical risk in Dallas, San Francisco, or Chicago, but I would put myself at a greater psychological risk since I would leave behind the network of my strongest supporters.

All this I explained to my father, crystallizing my decision to stay as I talked. I expected him to object, to at least encourage me to spend a few months in a distant city, but what he said was

"Well, if you think that's what's best for you, then that's what you should do."

I almost dropped the phone. That he trusted my brain-injured judgment confirmed to me that to him I was okay.

◆

I began coming to New York regularly on weekends, going to the theater with friends, eating out, relaxing in my apartment—doing the things ordinary people do, as if I had returned to that category.

In mid-October, I went to the New Jersey shore with Kevin. As noted, we had almost ended our relationship on April 15. On that day, both of us had wondered where we were headed. I think he suggested dating other people, and I hesitantly agreed. We were in that passive state acknowledging that what's going on is pleasant, but there's no intensity. I wasn't sure how I felt about him, and he wasn't sure how he felt about me. The evening ended inconclusively: let's just see what happens.

Then, the attack. Kevin's visits to Metropolitan. Our nice times at Gaylord, our comfortable weekends in Montclair, and his dear, considerate, thoughtful, empathic behavior throughout. I know that how a person feels about you affects how you feel about him. Maybe his feelings toward me were different from what I had thought, and if so, how would that affect my own emotional state? Here it was six months later. I wanted to find out.

We sat on a park bench, looking out at the ocean. "You know that conversation we had the weekend before the attack?" I asked. "Have things changed since then? I mean, you've come to visit me, you've taken care of me—but have your *feelings* changed?"

They hadn't.

Kevin recently told me he didn't think it fair or appropriate for him to back off at a time when he felt I needed support. He acknowledged that seeing me improve helped him psychologically. He had waited for me to bring up the subject of our previous discussion, but now that I had—well, frankly, it was time to move on.

I appreciated his honesty. That I was just about to get out of Gaylord and reenter life might have had something to do with the timing of our talk, though I don't remember thinking this consciously. Still, I was relieved. Ahead of me lay tremendous challenges, even in the familiar environment of Salomon, and to be emotionally unencumbered would make the task slightly easier. I cared about Kevin, and I'm sure he cared about me. But we didn't love each other. He was right: it was time to move on.

◆

COMMUNICATIONS DISORDERS DEPARTMENT
PROGRESS REPORT   10/13/89

Trish has been receiving speech/language therapy services from 6/7/89–8/7/89 at Gaylord Hospital, and from 8/9/89 through the present time on an outpatient basis while residing at Traurig House.

The focus of therapy has been on improving speech, language and cognitive abilities. Trish has shown steady gains in all areas addressed. Auditory comprehension, reading comprehension and written expression are functionally intact. An ongoing goal is to increase the clarity and organization of Trish's expressive language skills. Trish is demonstrating gains in her ability to include pertinent information in her explanations, and for summarizing complex and detailed information in a clear, concise and cohesive manner.

The precision of her articulation has also been improving with only minimal imprecision evident occasionally on multi-syllabic words during spontaneous production.

Cognitively, Trish has demonstrated significant gains in all areas. Attentional abilities are good, as is memory functioning. Steady gains have been evidenced in organizational skills, problem-solving skills, and deductive reasoning. Mild deficits persist in these areas, however. Mild deficits are also noted in mental flexibility. Abstract and verbal reasoning skills and inferencing skills are judged to be functionally intact.

Continued speech/language therapy is recommended . . . to address the goals of increasing organizational skills, deductive reasoning skills, complex problem-solving skills and expressive language skills.

Arlene Schwartz, M.A., CCC-SLP

Good enough to let me survive in the frenetic, pressure-packed world of Salomon Brothers? It would have to be.

Chapter Seven

Reentry

My gait was still uncertain. I would yaw as I walked and often had to steady myself against a wall for support. I had to *think* about standing up. Descending steps was still difficult. My eyes would get tired, and while reading, I'd cover my right eye with my hand to avoid double vision. The scars around my left eye were still inflamed, but I decided not to cover them up with hair or makeup; they were what they were and were now part of me. My colleagues surely noticed, but since I didn't *see* myself as scarred, I didn't carry myself that way. As for my cognitive faculties, I wasn't sure they could cope with the long days, the multiple assignments, and the deadlines.

Still, I was ready to leave Gaylord. I was sick of being weighed twice a week, tired of the constant testing to assess my physical and cognitive functioning, chafed at having to get prior approval for my weekend activities, and had begun to resent the many different psychotherapy sessions I attended. As several of my psychologists noted, I had a strong need to exert my independence, and independence in a hospital is a contradiction in terms.

I had gone from the helplessness of infancy to the skills of adulthood in slightly less than seven months, and I longed just to be me, to not be analyzed for it. I knew the hospital had to protect me, but my weekends away had filled me with a longing for full-time autonomy. If I needed help, I wanted to be able to choose my own helpers.

And so, on Saturday, November 11, 1989, I left the Gaylord grounds. The staff saw me arrive on a stretcher and now I was leaving on two feet. I felt excitement and fear at this passage. Though I was going back to the familiar surroundings of New York City and Salomon, it still produced anxiety. My escort was a friend from work, Michael Allen, the last person I remember talking to before the attack, who came to fetch me in his blue Corvette. Its sportiness seemed to me appropriate to my mood.

My departure wasn't announced; nobody wanted it to become a public event. And Michael drove me not to my apartment on 83rd Street, but to Battery Park City, across from the World Trade Center, where Salomon maintained one of its corporate apartments. I would stay there for the next few months, to avoid the press. As we drove into the parking lot, a tall, slim blond man with a kind face approached me.

"Miss Meyers?"

I had to think for a second. Lisa Borowitz had arranged for

me to be registered under a pseudonym, but it still sounded strange. "Yes, I'm Terry Meyers."

"I'm Jim Stone. I'll be looking after you." Jim's duties were to escort me to and from the office (we would sneak in through the underground garage), to accompany me on those rare occasions when I went out at night from my Battery Park apartment, and to drive me to my appointments during the day. He would wait until the appointment was finished, then take me back to the office or the corporate apartment. Salomon also had someone by my side when I went running on the weekends, which I usually spent in my old apartment uptown, my real home.

Jim and Michael got me unpacked and I moved in. Once I was settled, ambivalence emerged. I was finally independent, but I wasn't sure how I'd be received at Salomon or how I'd perform back at work. I didn't want to be "special," but sometimes special is nice. Freedom meant continuing the conflict between independence and need that even before the attack was part of my psychology. I was aware of my physical limitations and pretty sure I would be able to compensate for them. What I didn't know was how resuming my interrupted life would affect me psychologically and cognitively.

I worried about the press. Sooner or later they'd find me. I worried about being in the spotlight: How could I resume a normal life and continue to heal in privacy? I was nervous and felt that my family was nervous too, which probably made me more nervous. I wasn't physically afraid—the cocoon of Gaylord and being protected by Jim and safe inside Salomon made physical peril remote—but I was uneasy in a way I couldn't quite define. I had expected that leaving the hospital would be a huge relief. It wasn't.

I was to start work after the Thanksgiving weekend. Until then, I had time for a trip to Dallas for a couple of days to see my brother Bill. Lisa Borowitz arranged it, thinking the press surely wouldn't find me there. Bill had heard how much I'd progressed in the four months since he'd last seen me and probably expected a fully recovered sister to emerge from the airplane. The impact of my struggle with my double vision and with my balance along the Jetway was a shock to him and made him fear that "full recovery" might be overly optimistic, but he greeted me with a great big hug and kiss and we spent a happy few days together.

Back in New York, I went to the dentist, the hair salon, the grocery store, feeling free in the city even though Jim Stone was with me. On the Monday before Thanksgiving, I showed up at the office for a party in my honor where I was simultaneously fussed over and treated with studied casualness. A cake was waiting for me in Doug Lake's office. People asked, "How are you?" as though I'd been away for a week with the flu. Kevin, who worked in a different building, wasn't there (Salomon had offices in two buildings across the street from each other—one housed investment bankers, the other the trading floors and the research departments), but Pat Garrett was.

My parents came for Thanksgiving. We stayed with old friends in Paramus, near the house where I grew up. My aunt Barbara joined us. It was quite a celebration. This year of all years we had much to be thankful for. Neither of my parents was typically overly demonstrative, but on this day emotions ran high. I remember the innumerable hugs and kisses, the laughter, the excited talk, the joy of our being together. I gorged on turkey too, which, given my history, must have delighted them. On Friday, they stopped at my office so they could thank John Gutfreund and Tom Strauss personally for all the things that Salomon had done for me and for them. Even now, the company's generosity astonishes me. For the rest of my parents' stay we did tourist things, including a trip to the Christmas show at Radio City Music Hall.

Then, on Monday, I was back at my desk at Salomon, sharing the office with Peter Vermylen. Even though I wasn't a vice president, and only vice presidents and higher had offices, Salomon realized it was a less distracting environment than an open cubicle, and Peter graciously agreed to take me in. There was one hitch, though: Peter was allergic to flowers, and the dozens that arrived for me that day had to be moved.

It was a peculiar day. I wanted to be accepted back without fanfare, treated as just a member of the team who had taken a leave of absence. But this is difficult to do if you're accompanied by a guard and observed by your colleagues like some rare tropical fish. I was enormously self-conscious about being scrutinized, judged, evaluated, for "normalcy." Would I veer off course when walking down a hall, an obvious remnant of the head injury? Would I say something stupid? Not remember a word or important fact? It was the first day of school times a thousand.

I didn't know how my associates were relating to me, particularly those who had seen me in such bad shape at Metropolitan. The sense of being watched by my colleagues eventually subsided—they got used to me—but I continued to watch myself. Mostly, this was out of necessity. The office, like all offices, presented physical challenges for a brain-injured employee. I had to maneuver around desks, files, chairs, wastebaskets. Walking down a hallway while carrying anything could be dangerous. Any sharp turn posed difficulties. My balance problems meant I occasionally bumped into people or things; in one particularly humbling instance, I was seen knocking into a painting on the wall of the entry to the open trading floor. Such misadventures didn't happen often, but each time I felt embarrassed and frustrated.

My physical problems brought up issues of my childhood. I felt myself the little girl again, the "baby sister" held off by the extended arm of my big brother, the object of fun, fighting against a power I could not control. My deficits made me believe that people wouldn't take me seriously, always one of my greatest fears. At Salomon, my fight for control and need to watch every step was tiring at first, sapping energy from my everyday work, and served as a constant reminder of the attack. I was aware of everything I did, from how steadily I walked to doing a simple calculation on a computer; everything was a test to see how I was progressing.

❖

Two questions, or variations on them, came up frequently from people both inside and outside Salomon: "At what level, percentage-wise, do you think you're back?" and "Can you do the same things that you could do before?" I can understand why they asked these, but the questions bothered me. They implied that if I *wasn't* 100 percent, well, then I was an object of pity. I wasn't sorry for myself. I knew I would never be the "old" Trisha, that just as I had gone through another childhood of learning to walk, reason, care for myself, I had to learn to live in a new body with a new mind. Part of my adjustment was to feel comfortable answering these questions honestly. Physically, my abilities and limitations were easy to describe and I had little trouble doing so. Cognitively, however, the answer wasn't so simple or so comfortable; the mental deficits were subtle and at a high level, the very things I built my first life with: concentration, focus, word retrieval, staying on subject.

When I'd admit, for example, that I couldn't remember a name or come up with the right word, people would say, "Oh, I have that problem too." Their intention, of course, was to make me feel better, but, me being me, it didn't. I felt I shouldn't have these deficits. It was hard getting used to telling people what was "not perfect" with me, but I began to recognize that "different" doesn't mean "worse," and if I acknowledged deficiency in some area, I'd say, "But let me tell you about the gains I've made."

I remember an experiment I did in the first few weeks after my arrival at Gaylord. The things I had difficulty doing made me feel the loss of function that follows a brain injury. One night, while watching TV in my room, I thought, "What if a brain injury *improves* some skills, knocks the brain cells around in a way that allows you to do something you couldn't do before? Why is it always assumed only deficits will result?"

I had always dreamed of being a rock star but lacked the voice for it. Now I decided to sing along with the next commercial jingle to see if my voice, post-brain-injury, would let me sing duets with Billy Joel. Guess what? I was still a terrible singer. But the idea that improvement was *possible* stayed with me.

◆

I was right. My brain could improve—and did.

When I was at Gaylord, the belief was that people with a brain injury had at most one to two years to recover; the progress made in that time was all they were probably going to achieve. Today, new advances in neuroscience have disproved this thinking. We know now that the brain has plasticity, that through use and challenge it can actually repair and rewire its damaged circuits. And by focusing, by endlessly working on the physical and cognitive exercises laid out for me, by pushing myself ever harder at Metropolitan, Gaylord, and when I went back to work at Salomon, that's what I was doing—instinctively stimulating and healing the wiring in my brain.

The attack left me with what's called a diffuse axonal injury—the severe blows to my head caused my brain to slam against the sides of my skull and damaged many of the nerve connections called axons. The bleeding, swelling, increased pressure, and lack of oxygen to my brain caused further trauma. Wiring all over my brain was affected. Everything had to be recovered. I had so much damage initially that the most basic parts of my brain were affected and I was in a coma. As my bleeding and swelling resolved, I became more alert but I couldn't do even simple tasks. Through my participation in rehabilitation, through constantly pushing myself to the limit, I was able to slowly regain tasks such as standing and walking. Eventually I learned to dress and feed myself.

The human brain is more complicated than any computer ever built. The wiring in the brain is structured so that higher level functions such as memory, attention, and concentration have more delicate and detailed circuits. It took more time to regain these skills since the so-called executive functions—

memory, concentration, decision-making—recover last, as they did with me.

The amount of recovery depends on the type and extent of the damage. If the wires are cut, the chance of recovery is small; if, as in my case, the wires are compressed or stretched, potential for recovery is greater. One hundred percent recovery is rare. But in my kind of injury, because I see that I continue to make improvements, I know *the process of recovery never ends.*

◆

My male colleagues were unfailingly courteous and kind, reinforcing my belief that men were not rapists, not attackers, but were good and supportive. We were wary with each other, going out of our way not to make the other uncomfortable by discussing the attack. And everybody waited for me to take the lead on how hard I wanted to be pushed.

The administrative work I was assigned was real, as opposed to the work I did at Traurig. But it wasn't too taxing. Salomon is not in the business of rehab therapy, but that's the role they initially played for me. I'm sure they were scared of doing anything that might cause any kind of relapse, and so they took it easy. I went to meetings, where I participated like every other member of the team, but I had no interaction with any of our clients for well over a year, and I was not assigned the kind of analysis and research that Peter Vermylen's memo to me at Gaylord had asked for. And whereas I used to arrive at work at seven-thirty and often stay at my desk for more than twelve hours, now I was getting in at eight-thirty and leaving at five-thirty, and that included at least an hour off for exercise.

My major job was to keep track of the expenses the Energy and Chemicals Group was supposed to be reimbursed for by clients. Like most firms, we charged for the little things, telephone calls, cab fare home if work for a client forced us to stay late, as well as bigger ones such as travel expenses. Our fee for work was of course negotiated up front, but we added expenses to the basic bill ("You owe us the $3 million agreed upon—plus expenses"). Each client had a code, and I had to be sure each expense was assigned, coded, and billed to the right client. I performed well—the Group's expense-recovery rate increased by over 20 percent—but I was restless, questioning my abilities, wondering whether I'd ever get back to full speed.

In December, a month after my return, Doug Lake told me I had become a vice president. I had been at Salomon for three years, including the time off at Metropolitan and Gaylord, and it's at the three-year point when decisions are made about an employee's future at the company. One could be made a vice president later—three years is not an ironclad limit—but the three-year vice presidency was used as a sign you were accepted. Salomon tended to have people come in as a class (mine was the class of '86) and take them through vice president as a class. It was a kind of point of no return: employees either rose rapidly or fell behind after that.

A vice presidency! Immediately I was visited by my Salomon demon. I'm not producing as much as I had before the attack, I thought, yet they're still paying me well, compensation for far more work than I was actually putting out. Once more my feelings were ambivalent. On the one side was "These people aren't idiots, and people *do* get fired"; on the other, though I enjoyed the special treatment, I didn't think I was contributing enough to merit the promotion. I didn't want to be a poster child. I longed to show them I was okay, the same person I was before the attack, productive and normal, as a way of thanking them for, among other things, paying my medical bills, providing private nursing, setting up the Gaylord "office," and taking such good care of my family. I wanted to *earn* my keep, not be given it out of their good nature. But of course, for many months, I couldn't. Strangely, as I got better, the doubts got stronger. I became impatient. I questioned my abilities. Was I being kept at this relatively low-level job because I wasn't capable of doing more?

After I had been back for a year and a half, I remember going to Doug and asking to be given responsibilities similar to those I had before the attack—part of a team that interacted with our clients—to work on a transaction. Only then would I know if I could "do the same things as I had before." "I'm ready," I told him, but he was reluctant to move me to actual face-to-face encounters because few of the clients were in the New York area (for the Energy and Chemicals Group, many of them were in Dallas or Houston), and I'd have to travel to be with them. He didn't think I was physically ready for it and was worried about security. It wasn't until 1992 that I worked on a live transaction with a client, a stock offering for the oil service company Reading and Bates. Because I hadn't done this kind of work since before the attack, I took on the more junior analyst role, crunching numbers.

◆

One of my concerns about being a rape and traumatic brain injury survivor was whether anyone I didn't know before the attack would want to date me. I never felt myself any less a woman because I'd been raped, but would I be less attractive to men because of what had happened? Was it a stigma I could overcome? If a man—Kevin—had known me before the attack, he'd know the kind of person I was and that my personality wasn't all that different—the core Trisha. But somebody new? Would the baggage be too great to see beyond?

Tim Moore, my apartment building's representative to my family when I was at Metropolitan, and later to me, became my new romance. We had met only once before the attack and didn't really know each other. He saw me at my very worst in the early days at Metropolitan and, like everyone else, was appalled by my condition. And he visited from time to time during my rehabilitation at Gaylord. Now we found we had many of the same interests, and we became friends and then lovers.

Since we lived in the same building—indeed, on the same floor—we fell easily into a relationship. When I met him, Tim, a Southerner by birth, was a hot dog vendor with a difference, a unique entrepreneur. He dressed in a tuxedo, took his franks to Fifth Avenue, set up an elegant cart outside the Plaza Hotel, and provided New Yorkers and tourists with what he claimed were the finest frankfurters in the world. Tim made a great success of it. Soon he was invited by Bloomingdale's to sell "Fifth Avenue Franks" in their Lexington Avenue store—he claimed that sales of the franks grossed more per square foot than any other department in the store—and later, with a partner, he set up a business in Atlanta where he ran a Fifth Avenue Franks at Macy's.

Hot dogs weren't my favorite food, but I liked almost everything else about him. He was tremendously supportive, a superb listener at a time when I was adjusting to life on the outside. We shared a love of exercise and often went running together on the weekends, sometimes as much as four to five miles. He kindly slowed his pace to match mine; I was still unsteady. More important, he was an introspective, spiritual man, a great admirer of the philosopher/historian Joseph Campbell, and with him I explored and deepened my belief that there was more to healing than medicine, that there was a strong connection between mind and body. I also saw that through my recovery, my eating disorder had resolved and I started to internalize the tremendous love and support I received.

Tim and I stayed together for four years, though, as with Ken, our relationship lasted longer than it probably should have. More and more Tim's business called him to Atlanta, and we mutually agreed to part. We were, we acknowledged, no longer growing together. But Tim was there during those many tough months of living and working in the world again.

◆

As part of my ongoing physical therapy, I was allowed use of Select Fitness, the executive fitness center to which several Wall Street businesses gave their senior management membership. Being a vice president wasn't good enough; I'm talking *senior* management. I would go there often at lunch hour and worked out regularly with managing directors from Salomon, Goldman Sachs, Kidder Peabody, Lehman Brothers, and partners from law firms like Sullivan & Cromwell. I suppose as a career move it might have been a good idea to try to ingratiate myself, but I didn't pay much attention to them. I was working to rebuild my body, improve my balance, and make sure I didn't fly off the treadmill. This happened a few times, to the horror of the staff, who knew my identity.

I did become friendly with the staff. In a sense, they were my post-Gaylord physical therapists and played a critical part in my continuing physical rehabilitation. They took a personal interest in my progress, and like my therapists at Gaylord, I trusted them. I felt comfortable exposing my deficits and accepting their help as I worked to regain what I'd lost. Liz and Jay, the owners, worked closely with me, and so did Bob, one of the trainers and my massage therapist. They all remain good friends. One trainer stayed away at first, a muscular black woman with short hair. Years later she told me that she had avoided contact because she was afraid that I might associate her with my alleged attackers, bringing back bad memories. But eventually Laura introduced herself to me and we began to work together.

On Liz's advice I took up weight lifting and one day, all of a sudden, discovered I had muscles where none had been before. This transformation gave me a sense of power and new self-confidence about my body. And gradually, I found that I didn't have to hold on to the treadmill handrails so long before I could run freely, and that my balance was improving. At Select Fitness both the trainers and I saw significant change continuing, and we kept at it.

I worked with Peter Rogowski as well, one of my physical therapists at Metropolitan. It was he who had helped me sit and swallow, had stretched my feet and legs for me in the first weeks after the attack, and had gotten me to stand and walk with assistance by the time I left. He had called me when I was at Gaylord to find out how I was and left his number. I asked him to work with me on the weekends, and he'd take me to the park in my neighborhood, where he'd have me roller-skate and stretch on the jungle gym. "You needed the fresh air, the oxygen," he told me recently, and introduced me to in-line skating to improve my balance. Skating among children at a neighborhood park was a humbling experience, especially when one parent commented, "You must be new at this." I smiled nicely, but fumed inside. "Can't you see how hard I'm working?" I thought. "Boy, I hope you don't discourage your kids like this." Peter was my outdoor trainer for four or five years and I still occasionally see him for help.

I had thoughts of moving to a building with an elevator and doorman, something my mother would have preferred since it might afford me greater protection, but I decided to stay where I was. Walking down and up the stairs to my fifth-floor apartment every day forced me to exercise muscles and brain connections aligned to my problems with balance.

◆

Just as my physical therapy continued, so did my psychotherapy. My brothers told me how much they had benefited from talks with Iona Siegel, director of the Sexual Assault and Violence Intervention (SAVI) Program at Mount Sinai Hospital in New York, when I was at Metropolitan.* Iona had provided such

---

*SAVI provides around-the-clock emergency room advocacy in nine Manhattan and Queens hospitals; free confidential counseling to survivors of rape, sexual assault, incest, and domestic violence, and to their families and friends; and public education programs throughout New York City. I cannot praise its work too highly.

effective counseling to my family that my brother Steve wrote her saying, "To whatever extent Trisha's recovery can be linked to the support she received from family and friends, that support would not have been nearly as strong or focused without the tireless help of you and SAVI." My brothers encouraged me to see her when I got back to New York. Gaylord also recommended I continue receiving psychotherapy, and early in 1990, I made an appointment, the first of many, with Iona. A brilliant and compassionate woman, she built the SAVI Program virtually single-handedly and runs it with the boundless energy of those who have devoted their lives to survivors' causes.

Iona specializes in helping survivors cope with the trauma of sexual assault, which often includes symptoms of posttraumatic stress disorder, such as nightmares, flashbacks, general anxiety. Since my lack of memory lessened the chances of my experiencing PTSD, and because I had suffered a severe head injury, she and I both recognized that I might be better served by a psychotherapist with a medical degree who could provide more comprehensive therapy. She recommended a psychiatrist, Stuart Kleinman. For a while I saw Iona once a week and Dr. Kleinman twice, and they coordinated my treatment. Eventually, though, I saw only Dr. Kleinman. In my first weeks with him, just before the first trial was about to begin, we worked primarily on the relaxation techniques I would need if I became stressed on the witness stand when I testified. After all, I would be in the enclosed space of the witness box and possibly be cross-examined by a hostile attorney, forced to reply to questions that I didn't necessarily want to answer.

After the trials, I continued to work with Dr. Kleinman for six years, valuable sessions that were a large part of my overall healing. He and I used the trauma to enable me to take stock of my entire life. Among other things, psychotherapy let me see my compulsive running as a symptom of psychological demons that had haunted me for years.

The running provided fulfillment of an unconscious psychological need. Before the attack, I was feeling pretty small at Salomon. In my mind, I wasn't excelling at work. I found out I was being paid in the middle range of people who came into the firm when I did, and to me this yardstick confirmed my sense of mediocrity. But feeling small started earlier. So did running.

With Dr. Kleinman, I began to see that I had internalized what I thought my parents expected of me. They had never said, "You'd better be the smartest and the best," but they were accomplished, successful, bright people, and I felt I had to be at the highest level because they were too.

I discovered I had developed a harsh inner critic. That I could never please this critic led to feelings of inadequacy. I saw how my critic had created a competition—me against me—I could never win. My critic measured me against others as well, and no matter how great my accomplishments, they always counted less. As my success in school and work took me to more and more competitive environments, the feelings of inadequacy continually increased.

Running combated my inner critic. Here was a field in which I had stamina, endurance, "heart"—and the feeling of accomplishment when I finished a run was compensation for my "inadequacies" in other areas. So I ran too much. I ran compulsively. I *depended* on it.

Dr. Kleinman helped me quiet, not silence, my inner critic, who still pops up occasionally. I slowly developed a more mature view of my parents. I *knew* that they only wanted me to be happy, and I became more comfortable with them, especially my mom. Most of all, I became more accepting of myself.

No matter the motives, conscious or unconscious, it was my responsibility, my choice, that I was in Central Park that night. I don't feel sorry for that choice or for myself, and I don't blame myself for having made it. Though I never, ever imagined the run would have the result it did, I understand why I was out there.

I learned as well that I didn't have to do everything by myself, that it was okay to ask for help and welcome it when it was given; and to be easier on myself when I made a mistake or wasn't "the best."

I stopped seeing Dr. Kleinman not because all my issues were resolved—like everyone else's, they never will be—but because for several months I had been feeling that I was at peace with the attack and with the rape and could deal with old demons by myself.

The media coverage continued. My alleged attackers were to be tried in the early spring of 1990, and with several exceptions, particularly on the anniversary of the attack, newspaper attention was diverted from my recovery to the complex issues faced by both prosecution and defense. No forensic evidence conclusively linked any of the accused to the attack on me. The prosecutors were basing their case almost entirely on the statements made by defendants. Through their lawyers, the teenagers who had confessed were recanting and claiming they were coerced. And most troubling and sensational of all, DNA tests on semen found on one of my socks matched none of the defendants', indicating that there was someone out there who hadn't been caught.

"Jogger Trial Stalled" screamed the New York *Daily News* on April 3. "New Evidence Delays Jogger Trial" ran a headline in *Newsday*, also on the third. The trial was delayed seven weeks so that DNA tests could be performed on the newly discovered stain. The prosecutors decided to go ahead with the trials even though the DNA matched none of the defendants, leaving this unexplained fact hanging.* The first trial was rescheduled to begin on June 13. Jury selection commenced on June 11.

The media clamored for my reaction to the upcoming trials, but Salomon protected me. Because I was brought in and out through the underground garage, I never saw the press who crowded the front of the building, and the firm requested that none of my colleagues answer questions about me. All inquiries were referred to Corporate Communications.

I kept up with the news, just as I had at Gaylord during the pretrial hearings, but I didn't get caught up in it. By the time the delay was granted and a new trial date set, I knew I would be testifying, but there was nothing I could do in the meantime, so I kept up my regular routine.

One event did move me deeply. I had heard that the Guardian Angels were doing something in support of me in Central Park the day before the trial started, so I went to investigate. When I got there, I was handed a blue ribbon and a flyer:

---

*The mystery was not cleared up until 2002, when Matias Reyes admitted to the attack and his DNA matched the DNA of the semen on my sock, as well as on the cervical swab taken after the attack.

> *Guardian Angels Urge*
> *You to Support the*
> *Central Park Jogger &*
> *Show Unity with All*
> *New Yorkers—Wear Blue*
> *Wednesday, June 13, 1990*
>
> Stand up for what's good in
> our city! Show support for
> this innocent woman, as well
> as the countless other
> female & male crime victims
> of all races and ethnic groups.
> It's not a question of Black
> vs. White, it's about what's
> wrong & what's right.

I was surrounded by people taking the ribbons and pinning them on, and I did so too. I was, of course, unknown to them, just one of the crowd standing up for right in the face of wrong.

In a few weeks, I would be on the witness stand, proclaiming those same values in a far more individual way.

Chapter Eight

The Trials

The fact that thirteen years after the assault a man claimed he alone raped and beat me, rather than the five who were tried and convicted for the crime, doesn't affect the degree of my injuries, the lasting damage the attack left, nor the story of my rehabilitation. Even though the convictions were vacated, the trials are part of that story. They took place in the summer and fall of 1990. I briefly participated in them. This chapter is about that time, not this one.

◆

It is approximately ten paces from the witness entrance of Courtroom 763 at 111 Centre Street, New York City, to the witness box, and you have to climb two steps when you get there before you can sit in the witness chair. On July 16, 1990, I walked those paces and climbed those steps, to testify in the trial of three of my alleged attackers. There would be a later trial of two different defendants, and I would make the same passage to testify again.*

I know the number of paces and steps because I recently revisited the scene. On the sixteenth, I was not conscious of such minute details; my focus was on what I was about to say and how I would say it. I was aware, however, that the jury was on my left, the judge on my right, and that the benches at the back of the courtroom were full of spectators, among them many of my friends, whose presence was enormously comforting, and many of the friends of the defendants. Ardith was there, and Lisa Borowitz, and Father Bill's brother-in-law. In front of me stood prosecutor Elizabeth Lederer, the assistant district attorney. She told me to concentrate on her and her questions when I spoke. To her left sat the defendants and their lawyers. I forced myself to look at the accused, determined to let them know that they hadn't defeated me. My purpose was to help in the service of justice. Above all, if they were guilty, I wanted to make sure they never did anything so awful again. I only glanced at them; it was

---

*The prosecution had strategic reasons for requesting that certain defendants be tried together in separate trials, a request the judge granted over objections by defense counsel who pressed for separate trials for their clients. A detailed description of both trials, as well as the cases against the accused that led up to them, can be found in Timothy Sullivan's book *Unequal Verdicts* (Simon & Schuster, 1992).

enough. Then I turned my attention to the court officer and put my hand on the Bible.

"Do you swear to tell the truth, the whole truth, and nothing but the truth?" he asked.

I wanted my voice to be strong when I answered, to show both that I was not afraid and that I was physically and psychologically strong, even in this supercharged situation. "I do," I said, and I'm told that my voice then, and in my subsequent testimony, carried clearly throughout the courtroom.

◆

As I've noted, the question of whether I would testify was a major issue throughout the preceding months. My family was adamantly opposed. They had been through the anguish of the media bombardment when I was attacked, and they feared that a new frenzy over my appearance would be traumatic for me. "You don't have to do this," they said. "You can't identify who did this to you. What good would your testimony do?"

It wasn't only my family. In the spring of 1990, Larry Pedowitz, who had replaced Mary Jo White as my attorney, went with me to Gaylord to review the psychiatric reports and to talk to some of the doctors there about their view of the risks associated with my testifying. He talked as well to Dr. Bookheimer, who had left Gaylord the previous summer, and to Iona Siegel of SAVI at Mount Sinai. "All of them agreed there was risk," he told me later. "They were concerned that testifying could have an emotional impact on you, either immediate or well after the trial. Their concerns were not that your short-term memory would be activated—you were never going to relive the horrific event you had lived through. Rather, they were worried that you might suffer some trauma as a result of being in the courtroom, being asked potentially embarrassing questions by people you had no reason to like.

"Elizabeth Lederer had advised us that she had confessions from the defendants, that they were reliable confessions, and as a consequence you could reasonably believe they were guilty. I could certainly see, from your perspective, that being forced to be in a place with boys who had actually admitted to doing this horrible thing was not aimed at doing any good for you."

All this made me reluctant to testify. I took Dr. Bookheimer's and my family's concerns seriously, though my gut feeling was that testifying wouldn't trigger anything cataclysmic. Initially Larry agreed with my staying away. He and Susan Bookheimer met with Elizabeth, and Dr. Bookheimer repeated what she had said about the dangers to me in a court appearance. "I thought it was a useful meeting," Larry said. "I don't think she gave us a reaction immediately. Rather, Elizabeth asked to talk to you directly. She conveyed the notion that she really thought it was important for you to testify."

If what "important" meant was merely showing off the injured victim to gain the jury's sympathy, neither Larry nor I would have agreed to it. But there were critical questions only I could answer. When and what course I usually ran in Central Park. Who my boyfriend was and when we had last made love. (An insane theory was already being bandied about that my boyfriend—Kevin—had caused my injuries during rough sex, an argument that harkened back to the infamous "preppie murder case," in which a young man had strangled a woman during sex in Central Park, ruled on in the spring of 1988.) And only I could testify to the extent of my injuries *now* to make it clear to the jury that even though I looked pretty good a year and three months later, I still had suffered serious cognitive and physical disabilities. That is, the prosecutors wanted the jury to understand the *consequences* of what had been done to me, and to be told it directly rather than from some doctor, psychiatrist, or coworker.

Elizabeth explained this passionately and persuasively to Larry and to me in a later meeting. She assured us she would make me familiar and comfortable with testifying. She would be my champion in court and would try to ease my way through her questions as gently as possible. And she *needed* me. But if I didn't want to testify, she would certainly understand.

Part of my decision rested on my knowledge that I had nothing to hide. Yes, Elizabeth would ask me details about my sex life with Kevin, but some of the information had already appeared in the press. I believe in responsibility and wanted the defendants to take responsibility for the actions they had confessed to if they were guilty. Though I held little rancor for them as individuals and had no desire for vengeance—I did not know them, could not recognize them—I nevertheless wanted to tell them, "If you tried to put me down, you're not getting away with it."

I was torn between my family's opposition and my own sense of justice. Elizabeth had reached out to me, was sensitive to my feelings, and had carefully listened to my doctors and therapists. I don't think she would have asked me to testify if she thought it would do me harm. If I didn't participate in the process, I told myself, I would feel guilty that I hadn't done my part, that I hadn't acted on what I felt was my responsibility. In the end, the risks of silence outweighed the risks of testifying. So after weeks of thought, I did what my gut told me was right.

I said yes to Elizabeth.

◆

By the late spring of 1990, I was aware of my alleged assailants and the graphic statements some had made on videotape when they were questioned by investigators and Elizabeth Lederer. Like these:

> [Defendant] ran in back of her and she looked back at [him] and she started running a little fast. [Second defendant] came out towards the front and grabbed her from the front. . . . Beginning right there, that's where they started a little rape. Then they pulled her all the way down . . .

> He was covering her mouth. Every time she was talking, he was smacking her, saying "shut up bitch." He kept smacking.

> I grabbed her arm. Then we took turns getting on top of her . . .

> [Defendant] and [Second defendant] picked up a rock. . . . [Defendant] hit her in the face with a rock. That's what knocked her out, definitely knocked her out. . . . When they got off of her . . . when they started cutting her, when they started hitting with the bricks, I see blood scattering, I moved out of the way. Blood was scattering all over the place. I couldn't look at it no more.

This last was quoted in *Newsday,* which also ran photos from the videotapes, showing one defendant demonstrating how my arms were pinned during the attack and another pointing to where I had scratched him. The accompanying article reported that three defendants "all admit to participating in the gang rape."*

Elizabeth and Larry did not have to tell me about the defendants. I didn't meet with Elizabeth often (I remember only one time before each trial), since she was concerned that too many meetings would imply collusion between us and thus give the defense the opportunity to claim my story was rehearsed or manufactured. Rather, Larry did most of the prep work.

"We anticipated that the defense lawyers, if they were smart, would not cross-examine you—certainly not in the first trial— because it would likely evoke sympathy for you," he explained later. "But we were also realistic enough to know that there was a possibility that one or more of the lawyers would just feel that it was in his client's interest to ask questions. My objective was to make you comfortable with anything that might come at you."

Lots did come during the second trial. But I was prepared for it.

◆

Throughout this period, I was, of course, continuing with my work at Salomon and my relationship with Tim. I remember

---

*Defense lawyers argued that the confessions should not be used at trial, claiming that they were obtained improperly. The court, however, ruled that the statements were admissible.

thinking that my brain was overloaded; I couldn't stop wondering what testifying would be like. It's perhaps for that reason that the two trials are mixed together in my mind. Was I nervous? Not about what I would say—Elizabeth went over what she would ask me about—but that I would be perceived as damaged. I determined that when the time came, I would focus all my attention on Elizabeth.

Focus. It was an act of will that had returned and served me well at Gaylord, and I trusted it to see me through now.

◆

Elizabeth wanted to make sure I would not be plagued by the press, so she arranged to put me on the stand as the first witness of the day. Larry and I were picked up and delivered to the courtroom early in the morning before the press congregated. At six-thirty, we were taken in an unmarked police van with one-way windows (I could see out; no one could see in) to the underground garage beneath the courthouse from which prisoners are often escorted to their trials and, in a different elevator, judges make their way upstairs. Larry and I were taken in the judges' elevator to an unoccupied judge's chamber near the courtroom.

Soon Elizabeth arrived to calm me down in case I was nervous. Actually, *she* was nervous. Who could blame her? First of all, she wasn't sure that I'd be able to stand up to the pressure of a public appearance under such charged circumstances. But perhaps more important, for weeks she had been forced to make her way to the courtroom, under police escort, through a phalanx of angry supporters of the defendants—an extremist fringe of a group that called themselves "the Supporters"—who shouted "witch," "bitch," "white devil," "whore," and "slut" at her with each step she took and then congregated outside the courtroom so they could continue the abuse during breaks. The renowned black activists Al Sharpton and Alton Maddox, who were often present, did not add to the vilification, but their inflammatory rhetoric did nothing to calm the situation. Also in the crowd were members of the Guardian Angels and a large feminist group—*my* "supporters"— hordes of reporters, and random curiosity seekers come to see the show. Judge Thomas Galligan kept firm control of the courtroom as the trial went on, but he could do nothing to stop the abuse of Elizabeth outside it, and her tension as she spoke to me then was painfully obvious—she told me later she began to suffer from excruciating migraines.

Elizabeth left to take her place in the courtroom and call me as a witness. The summons came a few minutes later. "Oh, my God, here we go," I remember thinking, as a kind, considerate security officer named Nick escorted me toward the courtroom. I was walked down the hall to the witness entrance. "Every eye in the courtroom is going to be on me," I thought, *and they're going to be looking for something that's wrong. They're going to be looking to see if I can walk straight. They're going to be looking to see my scars. They're going to be listening to see if I can complete a sentence.* I didn't wonder what it would be like with the defendants in the room; I'd thought about that and discussed it with my therapist and felt calm about it. While I can't say that I didn't feel anything about the rape, their presence was not the overriding issue.

I knew what I had to do. "She wore a bright purple suit and a thin gold chain around her neck," the *New York Times* reported. "Her sandy blond hair was cut short and parted on the side, revealing the scar around her left eye—a scar caused, the prosecution contends, by repeated blows from either a length of pipe or a rock."

I was sworn in, seated. Elizabeth's eyes met mine. She smiled. I felt safe.

Yusef Salaam, Raymond Santana, and Antron McCray were the accused at the first trial, each with his own lawyer: Peter Rivera represented Santana, Robert Burns represented Salaam, and Michael Joseph represented McCray. I knew all the names, of course, for Elizabeth or Larry had told me about them, and they were mentioned in all the newspapers, but the faces meant nothing to me.

My testimony was essential to Elizabeth because one of the pieces of evidence that would be used by the defense was the discovery of semen on the crotch of my running tights. Its DNA matched none of the defendants', but rather Kevin's, possibly lending credence to the defense theory of "rough sex." Through me, Elizabeth had to explain how Kevin's semen got into my tights—and, more crucially, when.

Her opening questions concerned my age, place of birth, place of upbringing, my move to New York, and my position at Salomon. Then she turned to my running: at what time of day, location, whether I ran alone, and the usual route I took in Central Park. She asked me how much I remembered of April 19, 1989, when my memory returned after the attack, how long I stayed at Metropolitan, and when and how I was transported to Gaylord.

Q. Ms. Meili, I'm going to show you what's been marked as
   People's Exhibit 33 in evidence. . . . Have you had an
   opportunity to see People's Exhibit 33 in evidence prior
   to today?
A. Yes, I have. . . .
Q. You recognize People's 33 in evidence?
A. Yes.
Q. What do you recognize this to be?
A. That's the shirt I used to wear.
Q. Prior to April 19 of 1989, what color was this shirt?
A. It was white.

(The shirt had been drenched with my blood, as though I had
showered in it, and was now completely covered with reddish
brown stains from both my blood and the mud I had lain in. Elizabeth had showed it to me earlier, so I was prepared for the sight,
but still I recoiled. If any one thing demonstrated the viciousness
of the attack, the sheer brutality of it, it was that shirt.)

Q. I'd also direct your attention to a large hole and two
   small holes that appear in People's Exhibit 33 in
   evidence. Were those holes in the shirt the last time you
   saw it prior to April 19, 1989?
A. No, they weren't.
Q. I show you what's been received in evidence as People's
   115. Have you had an opportunity to see People's 115
   prior to coming to court today?
A. Yes, I have.
Q. Were you able to examine these tights at that time?
A. Yes.

Q. Do you recognize those tights?

A. Yes, I do.

Q. What do you recognize them to be?

A. Recognize them to be the tights that I would go running in.

Q. At the time you last saw them, did they have the holes cut out of them that appear to be in court today?

A. No.

(I identified my shoes and socks as well.)

Q. Ms. Meili, do you recall the days prior to Wednesday, April 19 of 1989?

A. Yes, I do.

Q. Did you have sexual relations with anyone prior to April 19 of 1989?

A. Yes, I did.

Q. When was that?

A. On Sunday, the sixteenth of April.

Q. Other than the morning of April 16 of 1989, did you have sexual relations at any time between the morning of April 16 of 1989 and the time of your last memory, at approximately 5 P.M. on April 19 of 1989?

A. No, I did not.

Q. Who were you with on the morning of April 16, of 1989?

A. Kevin O'Reilly.

Q. Who is Kevin O'Reilly?

A. He is my boyfriend.

Q. Did you use any form of birth control on that day?

A. Yes, I did.

Q. What did you use?

A. I used a diaphragm.

Q. Did you follow the prescribed use of a diaphragm when you used it on the morning of April 16, 1989?

A. Yes.

MR. JOSEPH: Objection.

THE COURT: I'll allow it.

Q. Did you also use the necessary precautions required for the removal of the diaphragm after you inserted it on that day?

A. Yes.

Q. Did you have vaginal intercourse on that day?

A. Yes.

Q. Did you have any other form of intercourse with Kevin O'Reilly on that day?

A. No, I did not.

Q. On the morning of April 16, did you have occasion to go to Central Park?

A. Yes, I did.

Q. At approximately what time, do you recall, did you go to Central Park on that day?

MR. JOSEPH: Objection.

THE COURT: I'll allow it.

MR. BURNS: What date is this?

THE COURT: The sixteenth.

A. It was sometime between nine-thirty and ten-thirty in the morning.

Q. And would you describe for the jury the circumstances under which you went to Central Park on April 16 of 1989?

MR. JOSEPH: Objection.

THE COURT: I'll allow it.

MR. JOSEPH: May we approach on this, Judge?

THE COURT: Yes.

There followed a discussion at sidebar—a conference between the lawyers and the judge outside the jury's hearing. Through both such interruptions, this time and once during the second trial, I was led out of the courtroom through the witness door, and I sat on a chair close to that door waiting to be called back in. Tim was in the corridor waiting for me—his presence inside the courtroom might have been a distraction. I remember how happy I was to see him.

I discovered from reading the transcripts later that Mr. Joseph wanted to find out from Elizabeth what the purpose of the questions about the sixteenth were. They seemed to him irrelevant.

MS. LEDERER: The primary reason necessary to call Miss
    Meili at all at this trial [is] because semen had been
    found, identified through DNA testing, that matched
    her boyfriend in her running tights. She will testify that
    after having vaginal intercourse with Kevin O'Reilly on
    the sixteenth, she went to Central Park and wore the
    tights [on] which the stain was found.

MR. JOSEPH: That seems to be my objection. I don't know
    the relevance of her testimony concerning running in
    the park.

THE COURT: What is the relevance of her running in the
    park that day?

MS. LEDERER: She wore her jogging tights.

THE COURT: I understand that.

MS. LEDERER: I'm not going to ask anything about the
route she took. She had occasion to put on the jogging
tights, and that's how the stain everybody used to trigger
this attack to Kevin O'Reilly came to be on that day.

MR. JOSEPH: Number one, I think it's an incorrect
statement to say that everybody tried to connect Kevin
O'Reilly.

MS. LEDERER: I withdraw that.

MR. JOSEPH: I don't see the relevance of her running in
the park on April 16.

THE COURT: I don't see the relevance of the running, but
putting the tights on seems relevant. I'll allow it for that
reason.

All that probably took more time than my own testimony
when I was allowed back on the stand:

Q. Would you describe the circumstances under which you
went to Central Park on the morning of April 16, 1989?

A. We went to go running.

Q. And when you went running on April 16, 1989, what
did you wear?

A. I wore my black running tights. . . .

In her closing statement, Elizabeth pointed out the significance
of this interchange. The running tights I had worn on the sixteenth I also wore on the nineteenth. Some of the semen had
stuck to them, even after washing.

Elizabeth asked me to describe the physical impairments I

still suffered from, which I did. Then, gently, she asked one final question.

> Q. Miss Meili, as you sit here today, almost fifteen months after April 19, 1989, do you have any memory whatsoever of what happened to you in Central Park on the night of April 19, 1989.
>
> A. No, I do not.
>
> Q. Thank you very much. . . .

The entire testimony took twelve minutes.

◆

As I had expected, press from all over the country were there. No cameras were permitted in the courtroom, and sketches were allowed only after I had left it, so the newspaper reporters had a field day. While they were sympathetic, they confirmed my fears that they would concentrate on my injuries, focusing on what was wrong with me rather than saying that the way I looked, walked, and spoke was pretty darn good. What I read I saw as criticism, and the overheated prose stung.

"Jogger: She Was A Walking Crime Scene," headlined Jim Dwyer in *New York Newsday.*

> Beyond the words was the stark testimony of her flesh. A spindly uncertainty to her gait. Eyes wide and not moving together. The tremor on her slight frame as she raised her right hand and swore on the Bible to tell a truth that her mind would not summon and her body could never forget.

She rose, yesterday, triumphant if wobbly, from newspaper Jogger to Person, a woman with a real name and two aisles of loving friends who watched with the jury as she stepped from the witness stand and bumped into a chalkboard.

"The jogger was holding the court spellbound," Bob Herbert reported in the New York *Daily News.*

She didn't weep, she didn't shudder, and there wasn't the slightest note of self-pity in her tone. There was not one word she uttered that wasn't believed. This time the tables were reversed. She was the dangerous one. . . .

You noticed the walk. Unsteady. Tentative. I had seen that walk many times before, in buddies who had been wounded in Vietnam.

At the time, I chose not to read most of this coverage; a little went a long way. It was enough to let me understand the mood.

"Her walk told more than 1,000 words," wrote Charles Carillo in the *New York Post,* whose billboard-sized headline read "Lady Courage." But a different story (the tabloids featured multiple stories each day) reported on the reaction of the Supporters, and this one hurt.

Yesterday, after the jogger's dramatic appearance moved a packed courtroom, they still refused to see her as a victim.

Instead, they ridiculed and taunted her as she left the courthouse in a white van with tinted windows.

"She's an actress! That wasn't the jogger. Where's the

jogger?" said one black man who raced down the stairway hoping to confront the jogger on the street.

"More racist lies!" he shouted.

As the van rounded the corner, the crowd turned to reporters and spewed more wild accusations about the jogger, her past, and the night in the park.

"Why don't they find her drug dealer that she went into the park to meet?" barked a strapping T-shirted antagonist. . . .

"Where's Kevin O'Reilly? Where's the boyfriend who met her at 10 o'clock?" [a woman] asked. . . . Why are they trying to lynch these boys? Lynch the boyfriend!

"Lynch all her boyfriends! She had many of them."

One of the saddest aspects of the trials was that it was so quickly turned into a racial conflict. To me, the trials, as well as the attack itself, weren't about race, but about violating and savaging a woman and leaving her to die. When I spoke at a SAVI Advocate Training meeting years later, a Hispanic woman told me that she and many of her friends in Harlem were praying for me because I was a woman who had been assaulted.

The point is not race. So when my case is used to inflame racial hatred, my heart breaks.

◆

A crowd of dear friends greeted me after my testimony. A policeman had led them around the back so they could be there when I had finished testifying. Their embraces and assurances that I had done well were a balm. I would now fly to Dallas to stay with Bill and his wife for a few days while the press quieted down. I wanted simply to escape the building in my secret little van and get to the airport. When things calmed, I could return and get back to work as usual.

But "as usual" meant prepping for the second trial, scheduled to begin on October 22, this time of Kharey Wise and Kevin Richardson. A sixth, Steve Lopez, whom others in their confessions claimed to be prominent in the attack on me, had not confessed or incriminated himself. He denied any knowledge of the assault on me, but admitted to being in the park with the group. He struck a plea bargain after the second trial finished and was sentenced to one and a half to four and a half years on a robbery charge relating to one of the other attacks that night. Until the plea bargain was struck, I thought I would have to testify in a third trial—his—as well.

Larry and I went back to work. Because Elizabeth had warned us that Kharey Wise's attorney, Colin Moore, had a reputation for toughness and was likely to cross-examine me, and cross-examine me hard, we staged mock cross-examinations, trying to anticipate Moore's questions. "I asked the questions I could think of that a defense lawyer, even if he was out of his mind, might conceivably ask," Larry said. By that time, the jury in the first trial, after a ten-day deliberation, had rendered its verdict: the three were each convicted of rape and assault (though not attempted murder) in my case, and of two other assaults, one robbery, and riot,* while they were in the park. This meant that cross-examination was all the more probable.

---

*Since each was under sixteen years of age, the court set aside the convictions except for robbery and rape.

During the first trial, it had been decided that Larry would not be in the courtroom, since Elizabeth wanted my focus solely on her. But now he planned to attend, and he was with me again when we were picked up early by the van and driven to the underground garage. We walked to where I would wait until called, this time a witness room on the floor above the courtroom.

James, a resident of my building who had seen me in the staircase as I was leaving for my run the night of the attack, came into the room. I don't remember whether he had already testified or would testify after I'd finished, but what he said would set the time of my departure for the run and thus establish that the attack could not have taken place earlier. There were policemen there too, though I was not sure whether they were witnesses or guards.

I remember a feeling of palpable tension. In this trial, I would be facing a hostile attorney, and all the playacting with Larry couldn't tell me what his demeanor would be, or the extent of his antagonism. Elizabeth dashed in for a word of encouragement; she seemed harried, uneasy. The phone rang. A court officer picked it up. "Okay, we're ready," he said.

This time I was not worried what the spectators might think; I was too concerned with the prospect of being cross-examined. Again I looked briefly at the defendants, almost with a feeling of defiance.

I was sworn in and Elizabeth took me through my testimony, almost exactly as she had at the first trial. "I have no questions of the witness," said Howard Diller, Kevin Richardson's attorney. There was a momentary delay. For a brief moment I hoped that Colin Moore would decide, as the other lawyers had, not to question me either. But then he rose and approached the witness box, smiling at me, ingratiating, dangerous. This was not playacting, the way Larry and I had done it in the conference room; this was the courtroom, and it was real. I tried to remember Dr. Kleinman's techniques for remaining calm, but Moore was already before me. My heart rate increased to match my fear.

I remember wondering how a man—any man—could choose to represent someone who had confessed to such a heinous act, having said "this is my first rape" on the videotape of his confession.* Intellectually, of course, I believe that everyone is entitled to a legal defense. Nevertheless, I was enraged. The accused had never seemed real to me—part of my capacity for distancing as well as that I didn't remember the actual event. But standing before me, Moore personified a continuation of the attack. I once again felt assaulted.

I recall him saying something about how bad he felt over what had happened. Not believing him, I wanted to ask, "Are you sincere?" But I remembered Larry's instruction "Just answer the questions," and I kept silent.

He began by attempting to show that my injuries were not as bad as I'd made them out to be. It made me angry, because I was proud of how far I'd recovered; it was something to celebrate, not be penalized for.

Q. You are presently employed at Salomon Brothers; am I correct?

A. Yes, I am.

Q. In what capacity?

---

*Colin Moore contended, among other things, that his client's confession was coerced.

A. I am vice president of corporate finance.

Q. And does your work—what type of functions do you perform as vice president of corporate finance?

A. When companies desire to raise money by [issuing] either stocks or bonds, we represent them. And also, excuse me, if a company wishes to buy another company or sell part of itself, we also advise them in that process.

Q. And it's fairly complicated work, isn't it?

A. Yes, it is.

Q. Does it require any degree of mathematical calculations, figures, types of things like that?

A. Yes, it does. . . .

Q. As a matter of fact, you're fairly good at your job, aren't you?

A. I like to think so.

Q. Well, one doesn't become vice president unless one is fairly competent at one's job; am I correct?

A. Yes.

Q. Do you still go jogging?

A. Yes, I do, as part of my rehabilitation.

Q. How often a week do you jog?

A. I usually jog five or six days a week.

Q. And are you thinking of taking part in the marathon on Sunday?

A. No.

Q. Now, in terms of the place where you live, are you required to walk up steps to get to your apartment?

MS. LEDERER: Objection.

THE COURT: I will allow it.

A. Yes, I am. I do.

Q. How many steps do you have to walk up?

A. Four flights of steps. I actually never counted them.

Q. I see. Now, what about social activities? You participate in social activities, don't you?

A. I do, but usually not during the week because I still go to work fairly early, and because I go to a gym for a couple of hours a day. When I come home, I go to bed. . . .

Q. Do you drive a car?

A. No, I do not.

Q. Have you ever driven a car before?

A. Yes, I have.

MS. LEDERER: Objection.

Q. You don't wear any type of glasses, do you?

A. I wear contact lenses.

Q. Did you wear contact lenses before?

A. Yes, I did.

Q. And you still have to read a lot of books and things like that in relationship to your job, don't you?

A. Yes, I do.

Under Elizabeth's questioning, I had already explained how my injuries affected me. I was given no chance to repeat that now. Moore veered off into more intimate territory: my sex life. I had already answered these terribly personal questions for Elizabeth; now I had to do it again.

Q. Now, Ms. Meili, you indicated that you had a boyfriend, Kevin O'Reilly; am I correct?

A. Yes.

Q. And you had indicated that on the Sunday preceding

this, that you did have sexual relations with him; am I
correct?

A. Yes, I did.

Q. Now, you indicated that you had used a diaphragm; am
I correct?

A. Yes.

Q. And you had a distinct recollection of using a
diaphragm of that occasion; am I correct?

A. Yes.

Q. Now, after you—typically, after you use a diaphragm—
have you used a diaphragm on any prior occasion prior
to the Sunday—

MS. LEDERER: Objection.

Q. Preceding—

THE COURT: Objection sustained. Don't answer that
question.

This was Moore's first foray into making me out as a promis-
cuous woman, part of the "blame the victim" defense—*see what
a slut she is*—common in rape cases. But Elizabeth had shut off
that avenue—for the moment.

Moore spent a long time asking me about the route I usually
took when running (I had no memory of that night, but I probably took my regular course, since I had certainly ended up at
102nd Street). He was trying to muddy up the timeline, place
me at the site before his client could have been there. James, the
man in the stairway, would set the time I left my apartment
building—I, of course, couldn't. I don't know if Moore felt he
wasn't succeeding, or if he was satisfied he had succeeded, but
he again changed the subject:

Q. Now, Ms. Meili, you indicated at about four o'clock on the afternoon of April 19, you had received a call from a friend; am I correct?

A. Five o'clock.

Q. Five o'clock, right. And it had to do with a dinner date; am I correct?

A. Yes.

Q. And do you recall the name of that friend who called you?

A. Yes, I do.

Q. And who was that?

A. His name is Michael Allen.

Q. Michael Allen. Michael was a good friend of yours?

The question bothered me because Moore was obviously trying to make this appear like a date between girlfriend and boyfriend, which it was not. But I didn't know how to get the point across, so I simply answered, "Yes."

Q. Would you describe him as a very good friend?

Ms. LEDERER: Objection.

THE COURT: I will allow it.

I answered with a question for Moore: "What do you mean by 'very good friend'?"

Q. Well, had you dated him on prior occasions?

A. No.

Q. Have you been intimate with him?

His strategy was clear, and infuriating. I had taken a hearty dislike to Mr. Moore. "No!" I answered emphatically, letting my irritation show. But I shouldn't have said anything. Elizabeth was on her feet, probably because she didn't know what my answer would be, and there's nothing worse for an attorney. She needn't have worried.

MS. LEDERER: Objection.

THE COURT: Sustained. [He turned to me.] If you see the district attorney stand up, please don't answer the question. The objection is sustained.

Q. Now, you said he had called you about a dinner appointment; am I correct?

A. Yes.

Q. Now, you don't recall, do you, whether Michael ever did come to your house that evening, do you?

MS. LEDERER: Objection.

Q. Do you have any recollection of that?

THE COURT: I'll let her answer.

A. No, I do not. I have no recollection. . . .

Q. Now, when you went home that evening, before you went jogging. Do you recall if you met anyone in your apartment?

A. I have no recollection after that phone call.

Q. And also, you would have no recollection as to whether Kevin O'Reilly was in your apartment when you went home that evening; am I correct?

Even now, reading the transcript over, I get furious at his implication and remember my frustration that I didn't answer it fully. Kevin and I didn't live together, he didn't have keys to my apartment, and we rarely saw each other during the week because I often worked late and he got to his office at 6:30 A.M.

> A. I have no recollection, but I don't believe that he was because he was out of town on Tuesday night, and he was to get back Wednesday....

He had gone out West on business, and I remember that the time he was going to get back was on Wednesday evening. In fact, he left a message on my answering machine saying he had gotten home—I heard it months later, as I heard Pat Garrett's message when he called my empty apartment at 10 P.M.

> Q. Okay. But you don't recall if he perhaps came a bit earlier than he had indicated, do you?
> A. No, I do not.

Through a series of questions, he had me acknowledge that many of my friends knew the route I took and the time I ran when I went jogging. Then, for reasons still unclear to me, he established that I was conscious of my surroundings before I left Metropolitan, that I jogged on and off campus when I was at Gaylord, and that I went to an outdoor concert on the New Haven Green in July. Then, a surprise.

> Q. While you were in Metropolitan Hospital, do you ever recall saying to a nurse—do you ever recall saying the name of a boyfriend—

Ms. LEDERER: Objection, Your Honor.
THE COURT: Sustained.
Ms. LEDERER: May we have a sidebar, please.
THE COURT: Yes.

I was led out—no Tim to greet me this time; he was in Atlanta on business—while at the bench an argument took place. Moore claimed that a nurse at Metropolitan heard me cry out the name of a male friend and say, in effect, "You're not going to do that anymore."

"Who is this nurse?" Elizabeth asked. "Was this someone in charge of her care? Is this a document in the medical records? Is this someone who had any connection to her care at all? What is the name of the nurse?"

"The individual is very careful," Moore answered. "A friend of hers spoke to my investigator—"

Judge Galligan, plainly skeptical, ruled that Moore could ask if I had any recollection of anything I might have said at that date. "If she says no," he said, "that's the end of it."

I was called back to the stand.

Q. Ms. Meili, while you were in Metropolitan Hospital, do
   you recall saying certain things while you were still in
   the ward of the hospital?
A. When?

I knew I shouldn't answer a question with a question, but I was surprised and blurted it out, even as Elizabeth was objecting. Judge Galligan asked the question for me.

THE COURT: What period of time are you talking about?

Q. This would have been three or four days after you had been admitted to the hospital.

A. No. I was still in a coma.

I remember that some in the jury chuckled, but Moore, undeterred, kept trying to press the point, and the point that Kevin and I might have been fighting before April 19, but Elizabeth objected to each approach and the judge sustained her objections. Moore was working on the slut factor and the boyfriend theory simultaneously, amping up the sleaze quotient. I remember my rage at him. I just wanted to get out of there. I understood why so many rape survivors choose not to press charges.

Finally, he indicated Kharey Wise.

Q. Ms. Meili, I'd like you to look for a moment at this gentleman here. Prior to April 19, 1989, did you ever see him before?

MS. LEDERER: Objection.

THE COURT: I will allow it.

Q. Ms. Meili?

A. No, I do not recognize him.

Q. Thank you. And you never saw him in the park on the night of April 19, did you?

This was a question Larry had anticipated, and he warned me that I would have to look at Wise. I did so without feeling any particular emotion.

A. I don't recollect it.

MR. MOORE: Thank you. . . .

He asked a few questions about whether I had taken any memory rehabilitation specifically about the events of April 19. I told him I had taken several memory classes, but none focusing solely on the attack. I was told by my doctors, and still believe, that it would have been futile. Hypnosis and other memory-retrieval techniques wouldn't have worked either. The damage from the blow on my head made memory impossible.

Moore chose to look at it differently.

Q. Ms. Meili, do you have an interest in seeing that those who have—would it—what happened on the evening of April 19 was very—a very traumatic event; isn't that correct?

A. Yes, it was.

Q. And therefore, you would naturally have an interest in seeing that those who committed it are convicted; am I not correct?

A. Yes.

Q. Wouldn't it also cause you some concern if the wrong people, people who did not do that to you, were convicted?

A. Yes.

Q. Therefore, you would have an interest then in making sure that your memory is restored so that you would be able to identify those people who committed the crime; isn't that correct?

MS. LEDERER: Objection.

THE COURT: Objection sustained.

Q. So is it your testimony, Ms. Meili, that between April
   20, or right after the events and up to the present time,
   that you have not sought a memory reconstruction?

MS. LEDERER: Objection.

THE COURT: She has answered the question.

Q. Is that correct?

THE COURT: She has already answered it once.

MR. MOORE: Thank you.

THE COURT: Are you finished? Do you have anything
   else?

I took these questions as a personal attack because I knew what he was trying to do. I couldn't counter his attempt to show that something was morally wrong with me for not working hard enough to remember. Remembering is an impossibility, I wanted to tell him, but couldn't explain the medical reason that I had no memory, and so said nothing.

In her brief redirect, Elizabeth simply reestablished that I'd made no alternative plan to meet Michael that night and took me once more through the process of my recovery to emphasize how grave the damage was.

"Any additional questions?" Judge Galligan asked Moore. "No," he said.

I was excused.*

---

*Kevin Richardson was found guilty of each count of the indictment, but because of his age, the judge set aside all of his convictions except those for attempted murder, rape, sodomy, and robbery. Kharey Wise was convicted of sexual abuse, assault, and riot. As noted, these and the convictions of the other three defendants were ultimately vacated.

◆

Was it brave of me to appear in court when I didn't have to, as some have suggested? I suppose it was, though I didn't feel heroic, just that I was doing the right thing.

At the time, I left the courtroom believing that I was two-thirds finished with a duty I had reluctantly undertaken. My part in the two trials was over, and though I thought there was still one to go—Steve Lopez had not yet struck his plea bargain—I felt free now to redevote my energies to my job, my friends, my continuing rehabilitation. I was relieved to have the trials behind me but frustrated by my inability to answer some of Moore's questions the way I wished I could. Even today, when I think about the trial, I still see his face.

Chapter Nine

Reaching Out

It's 1990. Tim and I have just seen *Watermill*, a Jerome Robbins ballet choreographed for Edward Villella in 1972. It is a controversial piece. The main character, Villella, is looking back on his life as others act it out in slow motion. He doesn't dance conventionally at all, showing his emotions only through subtle movement. This was the return of both Villella and *Watermill* to New York City for the first time since 1979. "*Watermill* elevates stillness to an art form," one reviewer said then. I agreed. Villella's presence now, eighteen years after the premiere, made the hour-long performance speed by.

"Didn't you tell me you once got Villella's autograph?" Tim

teases as we begin our dinner at The Ginger Man, a restaurant across the street from Lincoln Center.

I blush, slightly ashamed of a young girl's crush that's clearly morphed into an older woman's crush. I think Villella's fantastic. As a child, I had seen him perform several times with the New York City Ballet and fantasized dancing a pas de deux with him. Just like ballerina Patricia McBride. "It was the only time I ever asked anyone for an autograph, and I've kept the piece of paper he signed it on ever since," I admit. "What made you think of it?"

"Because Villella's sitting at that table to your right."

I look. It's true! I drop my fork. He is with a group of five people, all talking animatedly. Villella looks—beautiful. I could go up to him now, I think. Tell him how wonderful he was tonight and how I watched him perform as I grew up. Then I'm overcome with shyness and am loath to interrupt his meal. I'll wait till he goes to the men's room, I think, and intercept him.

But Villella doesn't get up, and Tim and I finally decide to leave.

◆

My story of lost opportunity may not be dramatic, but for me it's significant. It's one of the first memories I have of a time after the attack that's not in any way connected to it—I see myself as an utterly normal fan frustrated because she didn't get a chance to talk to her hero. That I remember it at all thirteen years later shows its importance. The Trisha in that memory is not the Jogger, but simply a woman who loved ballet.

I longed to go back to being me—or at least to come as close to my previous self as possible. I wanted the same responsibilities at work, the same routine of quiet and normalcy in my personal life. I didn't want to be the source of attention or conflict. I also felt the start of a growing tension. I was changing—sand turning to glass in the heat of the aftereffects of the assault. A new part of me acknowledged that I would never be the same, and I wanted to express what that change had taught me.

My desire to use my ordeal in a positive way began as a whisper, slowly and without my full attention, as a kind of nagging just below consciousness. I recognized from the beginning, however, that this would mean giving up my anonymity, and that thought held me back. My priority was still to get better, and self-disclosure would make that more difficult. And I wondered about the reemergence of racial conflict that surrounded the case—I didn't want to be the "privileged white banker" again, the term some used as an insult to stir up passions. I also wondered how going public would affect that part of me that yearned for privacy, a return to my life of working, seeing friends, exercising. Yes, I knew I had something to share. But I couldn't yet define it. It didn't feel safe. I wasn't ready.

◆

Before the attack, I was so concentrated on work that pleasure was an afterthought. Now I began to develop a life outside of work and exercise. Tim, other friends, and I went regularly to shows, ballets, sporting events, museums. I saw Ray Charles, Roberta Flack, and Billy Joel (of course!) and free events in Central Park—Shakespeare and Pavarotti. I explored parts of the city that were new to me, and restaurants in Greenwich Village, Chinatown, and Little Italy.

And I became more and more interested in the connection between spirituality and healing. I reads books by Deepak Chopra, Spencer Johnson, Oliver Sacks, and Bernie Siegel, all of which, each in a different way, resonated with my experience of recovery. The reading, over several years, led to many "Aha"'s and confirmed my sense of the power of the human spirit. I wanted to share this, to shout it from the rooftops. On the fifth anniversary of the attack, I even drafted a letter to the *New York Times* to let people know I was okay and to thank them for their spiritual support. But shouting from the rooftops means not only being heard; it means being seen. The letter was never sent.

◆

In the spring of 1991, my mother was diagnosed with multiple sclerosis, the kind called primary progressive. This means the decline is steady, the symptoms don't go away, and the patient usually doesn't respond well to drugs during treatment. The news was terrible for all of us. For her to get sick? Unthinkable.

Dad became the principal caregiver. As typical for him, he took to the job with wholehearted energy and love, though it became more and more difficult as Mom's condition worsened over the years and his fatigue mounted. Bill and Steve gave as much support as their families and jobs allowed them. I saw her as often as possible, though in the early nineties I was still unable to travel easily.

We spoke every week. She became open with me, talked about her sorrow and guilt at her growing dependence on Dad, her hopes for a miraculous development of a cure, and her increasing frustration over her inability to manage everyday life.

Her sense of balance deteriorated; she fell twice, breaking a wrist one time, a leg the other. Each time she fought back.

As I was getting stronger, she was growing weaker. I felt what she was suffering and encouraged her to exercise and eat well, knowing the benefits, and all the time watching her decline with anguish. I wished I could do more, give her the support she had given me. I forgot we were not always best friends, and our renewed closeness, I think, gave her comfort. It comforted me.

◆

In June 1991, I was asked to become part of a two-day presentation to new support-level employees about the "structures and workings of the firm" to give them a better understanding of the services Salomon provided. My talk was on the Corporate Finance Department; nine presentations describing other departments throughout the firm by nine vice presidents, directors, or managing directors made up the rest of the program.

Talk about a confidence builder. I was being asked to represent my whole division and explain to non-investment-bankers the intricacies of what we did.

Over the next three years, I went on recruiting trips to business schools and colleges such as Harvard, Stanford, and Yale, and as part of a team, I interviewed potential new employees. Though this indicated my colleagues were comfortable with my ability to represent the firm, I still continued to have misgivings about my professional skills.

I could do the work I was assigned in the Energy and Chemicals Group adequately and was made part of a team on a Reading and Bates stock transaction. But I found it hard work. I believed what I'd been hearing and reading during recovery: that when you're passionate about something, you accomplish things with greater ease and enjoyment; you feel it in your bones. I wasn't passionate about my assignments and began to sense I could offer more if I identified and located my passion. The pre-attack question of whether finance was the right place for me returned, surrounded by those altruistic whispers that had once led me to Zimbabwe. Should I try work more directly related to my recovery? No, I still needed the safe, familiar environment. Well, then, how about a transfer to another Salomon division?

I spoke to Doug Lake's boss, Denis Bovin, and he arranged interviews for me with the heads of different departments in the firm. At the end of 1994 I was offered a job as Business Unit manager for Fixed Income Sales. I did not become a bond salesperson or trader because I didn't have the necessary training, though it might have been exciting. Rather, my work was primarily administrative. I was responsible for creating and managing a budget for the sales force, maintaining the accuracy of the trading floor's hardware and technology, and looking out for cost-saving initiatives. I also became involved in a strategic analysis of sales force training. The work was different from anything I had done in Corporate Finance, and I was nervous about it. Could a brain-injured person cope with a new vocabulary, new faces and names, and new responsibilities? It was a big test, made more difficult by the physical challenges it entailed.

My new assignment meant that I spent the day on the trading floor of the most highly regarded unit of Salomon. Fixed Income Sales and Trading—i.e., government bonds, corporate bonds, mortgage-backed bonds—was the most profitable area of the firm and had a certain "Master of the Universe" mystique, as Tom Wolfe had characterized it in *Bonfire of the Vanities.* The floor itself, not as chaotic as the trading floor at the New York Stock Exchange, nevertheless held three to four hundred people packed together, their desks crammed with computer monitors and telephones, talking sometimes frantically on the phone to customers and shouting buy and sell orders across rows of salespeople. The place is an open rabbit warren: long rows of desks set in narrow, crowded passageways made maneuvering difficult even for somebody who could move steadily. And the cacophony of voices surrounding me sometimes made concentration a problem.

I may not have found my passion yet, but the work gave me a rush of adrenaline. My boss, Pat Dunlavy, was a wonderful manager who took the risk of hiring me and was steadfast in his patience and support when I made mistakes. I felt I was adjusting well, mastering new techniques and information, and making Pat proud of his choice.

But all the time thoughts intruded. Work was still the biggest part of my life, defining who I was. But I was doing midlevel work. Was I therefore a midlevel *person?* Had the attack really limited my potential? Was the firm just being nice to me, keeping me on sufferance because to let me go would be too cruel—and awful public relations?

Such self-doubt was another form of assault, an undercurrent running through my days. At the end of 1990, I had gone back to Gaylord for a neuropsychological evaluation to measure my mental capabilities, and the results troubled me. I had had two evaluations at Metropolitan when I was there, and another two at Gaylord, the last just before I left. Now, while my fifth evaluation showed that I had achieved "significant gains in cognitive capacity," deficits remained.

The way I saw it, if the repercussions of the attack meant I couldn't smell, or I'd have to always hold on to a banister when I walked downstairs, what difference did it make? I knew my physical limitations and lived with them. But intellectual ability was another matter. It was the trait my family valued most. I did too. It was my strength in high school, at Wellesley, and at Yale. *I've got to be the same as I was*, I felt. To learn through an objective test that I hadn't reached that goal was something I didn't want to face. So for many years, fear held me back from going for another evaluation. I was too afraid of what it might reveal.

This uncertainty contributed to my feeling of inadequacy. But something else was discomforting. I had nearly died. I had progressed from baby to adult in less than a year. I had been reborn. Yet here I was back at familiar Salomon, doing a job that could have been handled equally well or better by any number of people. We were no longer a good fit, Salomon and I. I was locked in the old battle between independence and security: Should I leave or stay? The voice that whispered that I should live differently was growing more insistent.

◆

When I ran on weekends—in the daytime and usually with others!—I often saw a police car parked at either the east or west side of the 102nd Street crossdrive. The attack had clearly led to increased vigilance on the part of the police department. Also, the New York Road Runners Club had launched a number of programs to improve park safety—"Safety Patrol," "Park

Watch," "Park Care," "Group Runs." The Road Runners community director wrote to me at Salomon, telling me about "all the positive programs that had been launched in response to your terrible ordeal."

Of course I was pleased. But I had made no proactive effort to help, and this added to my growing restlessness. I wasn't doing enough, I knew. I hadn't found the right connection.

I made a small start at filling in the missing piece by working for the Coalition for the Homeless, giving out sandwiches on Sunday nights. I'd look into the eyes of these often destitute men and women, trying to make contact, and occasionally succeeding. I also became a super fund-raiser—sitting on the trading floor among many who made millions, who could turn me down? I participated in swim-a-thons for the homeless, walks for MS, and was a spokesperson for Salomon blood drives.

I focused my attention on the organizations that had helped me, such as SAVI. I knew how they worked and I wanted as many people as possible to benefit from them. It was more than repayment. I was getting something too. The work was making me stronger, pointing me toward a new outline of what I wanted to do and whom I would become. In 1993, I joined SAVI's Board of Advisors to help them form strategies for expanding the program that had meant so much to me and my family. The work felt good, but it didn't quiet the whispers.

◆

My attitude about running had also changed. I still enjoyed the sport (though it was more difficult; my legs were heavier, my gait unsteady), and for healthier reasons. It was no longer my first priority, nor did I schedule my after-work events around it. I was happy at what I *could* do, at what I had "taken back," and grateful for the progress I saw nearly every time I went out.

Now there was a chance to put running to good use. In 1994, I decided to become a volunteer guide, like Nelson, who had been my coach at Gaylord. I would run with Achilles members at their Saturday morning workouts in Central Park. Often I ran with others who had a brain injury, and we talked about the challenges we faced. We enjoyed the companionship, the unspoken mutual understanding of our "differentness," and the pleasure of doing something the able-bodied did.

The founder and president of Achilles, Dick Traum, was an above-the-knee amputee who, in 1976, was the first such amputee to run in the New York City Marathon. In 1994, Dick decided to run the marathon again, but this time not with a prosthesis on his missing leg (which he had done ten times including one ultramarathon—sixty-two miles), but on crutches. He anticipated this would be a far more difficult feat, since his arms would have to bear so much of his weight and his hands might grow numb. He asked me to be his volunteer guide in the attempt. I readily agreed. For an elite male runner, the marathon takes just over two hours to complete. Dick's goal was to finish it in twelve. My tasks would be to help him if he fell; to apply Vaseline to his hands to prevent blisters (a danger even though he wore bicycle gloves); to massage and stretch his fingers every few miles to prevent numbness from using the crutches; to provide him with food (I carried a backpack); and to make sure he had a clear path among the other runners, especially at the water stops where the wet paper cups on the ground made the road treacherous as ice for someone on crutches.

We started at the Verrazano Narrows Bridge at 6:15 A.M. on a cold November morning with over fifty other disabled athletes and their volunteer guides, including a girl on crutches from Soweto, South Africa. (She and her guide were perhaps the first two women to visit New York City from that location.) There were many amputees like Dick, blind runners, stroke survivors, people with MS or cerebral palsy. The official start of the race was 10:50, but disabled runners who were likely to take more than eight hours to finish were sent off at the break of dawn. A faster disabled group started at 8:30. We would be passed by the elite runners at mile thirteen on the Pulaski Bridge between Brooklyn and Queens.

We started in windy darkness, with just a few officials to send us off, but soon the sun broke through, and a glorious sight it was! Brooklyn was quiet, but we walked near the curb of the road because traffic had not yet been stopped for the race. Soon spectators began to gather, applauding Dick and the other disabled athletes. Wheelchair marathoners whizzed past, greeting us with waves and huge smiles. At mile thirteen, we heard helicopters overhead, and the lead car drove by carrying the great marathoner Grete Waitz, this year one of the television commentators. Mayor Giuliani drove past too, pausing so he could shake Dick's hand. One spectator in the Bronx encouraged our slow pace by telling us, "Inch by inch, life's a cinch. Take it slow and it will happen."

The most difficult part of the race was getting across the 59th Street Bridge, with its long uphill climb and lack of spectators to cheer us on (they weren't allowed on the bridge). Dick and I felt tired and discouraged, but when we left the bridge, the jubilant, screaming crowd on First Avenue gave us a huge lift and we carried on. Dick fell near a water stop on First Avenue; another guide and I got him back up. He fell again less than a mile before the finish line. We paused for a moment. Dick, in obvious pain, encouraged by his wife, who had joined the race two miles before its end, continued. Sunset began to fall, replaced by darkness and the sliver of a moon, and this time a different, glorious sight was in front of us: the finish line. Crossing that line was a sensational moment for both of us. A surprisingly large crowd was still there, cheering. I applauded Dick, who finished in just under his twelve-hour goal. We hugged and stood under the finish-line banner holding our joined hands aloft in triumph. No medals were left, but we were given a "prize" anyway: the most delicious bologna sandwich I've ever eaten.

I had been training over the summer, running as many as ten miles, preparing for the 26-mile walk with Dick. I was surprised at how strong my body felt when I finished those runs, and my confidence and ambition rose. Now, simply *walking* the marathon was an exhilarating experience. What if I could *run* it, I wondered, be the athlete, not the guide? It was an intriguing prospect.

My activities outside Salomon grew. In 1995, I joined the Board of Directors of Achilles and became interested in a research project Dick proposed. Through working with disabled athletes, he had years of anecdotal evidence that people with traumatic brain injuries had a better self-image if they ran regularly than those who did not. I could see it in myself too. We approached Dr. Wayne Gordon, associate director of the Department of

Rehabilitative Medicine at the Mount Sinai Medical Center, with an idea: include TBI exercisers in the quality-of-life studies he had been doing with the disabled to see if exercise really made a difference. Dr. Gordon was intrigued and conducted a study of the benefits of exercising—jogging, swimming, or biking for at least thirty minutes three times a week—for people with TBI.

The results, published in a paper in *The Journal of Head Trauma Rehabilitation*, which I coauthored with Dr. Gordon and four other researchers, were dramatic. Brain-injured people who exercised regularly reported that they were less forgetful, could follow written and verbal instructions more easily, viewed themselves as healthier than nonexercisers even though their injuries might be more severe, were more often engaged in schoolwork, got around the community more freely, and, most important, were less depressed. The reasons are several. Sustained exercise requires concentration and focus, skills needed in daily life. Too, the more efficient use of oxygen might have positive effects on cognition.

This work, along with my efforts for SAVI, gave me considerable satisfaction. But when someone asked me what I did, I replied, "I'm an investment banker." That work defined me to the outside world. Less and less, though, it defined me to me. Who am I postattack? I continued to wonder. What path should I follow and where would it lead? Many people, I knew, confronted similar questions at some point in their lives. But unlike most of them I had to relearn how to walk and talk at the age of twenty-eight. I needed new self-definition to guide me through my second life.

◆

Physically, changes were going on that were easier to understand. I was eating! Not only salads and yogurt, but soups, fish, pasta, chicken, cookies. Exercise was important to me, but now I approached it simply as part of my ongoing rehabilitation. My muscles were meant for use, not overuse; I respected them. I didn't run at night or when I was tired. I cross-trained—rowing, biking, StairMaster, weights—stretched, rested.

And continued to run.

My marathon walk with Dick, which was surely one way to reach out to another, and my long runs that summer helped me understand the *point* of running. My attitude changed; my mindset changed. Running was no longer a psychological escape; now it was to set a goal and see if I could accomplish it. And if I couldn't, so what? *It didn't matter.* In the winter of 1995, calmly and with joy, because it was something I wanted to do without *having* to do it, I began to train for the New York City Marathon. And when fall came around, I believed I was ready.

The 1995 marathon was the coldest and windiest to date. This time *I* had an Achilles guide, Ted Rogers, one of the first people who had supported Dick Traum's vision for the track club. Ted and I made our way to the starting line along with over twenty-five thousand other runners. As we walked from the staging area to the start, we removed our warmer clothing, which was too bulky to run in, though it would be a while before the starter's gun went off.

"I'm *freezing*," I said.

Ted, a sixtyish athlete who was about to run his sixteenth consecutive New York City Marathon, had an idea: he gave me a bear hug. Ted's idea was so good that I noticed a few others around us adopting the "shared body heat" strategy, a lovely moment. Then, at last the starting gun sounded and we were off. A mob of people, us included, began to cross the starting line to the accompaniment of cheering crowds, band music, and the television crews flying in helicopters above us.

We went along pretty well until we approached the infamous twenty-mile mark, a time in the race known as "hitting the wall" to marathoners. I started to slow down. I'm not sure I'll make it, I thought. Ted noticed.

"You were an economics major at Wellesley, weren't you?" he asked.

I grunted a yes.

"Did you ever take a course with Carolyn Shaw Bell, the head of the department? I know her and admire her work."

"No." Talking was a struggle. "She was a tough professor and I avoided her."

"Well, tell me about some of the economic theories you learned."

I couldn't believe it! Is the man mad? I wondered. He's asking me for an intelligent response when all I can think about is whether I can put one foot in front of the other. It made me angry, but, brought up to be polite, I tried to answer him. My mind dug back to my macroeconomics courses—and suddenly I had broken through "the wall." My anger vanished. Another of this experienced marathoner's strategies had worked, and we resumed our old pace.

We reached 102nd Street, where the route of the marathon takes runners from Fifth Avenue into Central Park. For a second, I thought how close we were to the place where I was attacked, but then we saw Betsy, Ted's wife, cheering us on, and I forgot about it.

At this point, I noticed the official clock. Though time was not my primary goal—finishing the race was—I had thought, "Wouldn't it be something if I could make it in four hours?"— approximately my speed in previous marathons. But the clock read four-plus hours, and there were still three miles to go. "Let's get there under four and a half hours," I shouted, and took off, Ted following with a look of amazement on his face.

I was on familiar ground here. I knew every uphill, downhill, and curve of those last miles, and it felt great to run them. The energy that had been sapped by the race returned. My legs felt light, pliable. I had reclaimed "my" park. *I knew I would finish.*

Six and a half years after I had nearly lost my life in this park, had lost 75 to 80 percent of my blood, had nearly lost an eye, had lain in a coma from which some doctors believed I would never emerge—indeed, after doctors had predicted I would never regain my physical or mental capabilities—I crossed the New York City Marathon finish line in four hours, thirty minutes, and one second, and there's a picture on my desk of me crossing the line with the race clock above me to prove it.

Ted and I hugged again. I was hungry, tired, and overjoyed, though there was one deep letdown. My parents had come in from Pittsburgh to spend the five days surrounding the marathon with me, and my father stood at the southern end of Central Park so he could see me among the runners. My mother was now too debilitated with MS to stand for any length of time in the wind and cold. Somehow, my dad and I missed each other. It was horribly disappointing for both of us, and particularly tough for Dad. I was, after all, "his girl," and he had been through agonies, what with the attack on me and my mother's MS.

That night, though, I would meet my parents for dinner, and

we would celebrate my marathon. There would be no reason for me to run another. Soon after, I gave the medal I earned for finishing the race to my mom, in the same spirit the man from White Plains had given his to me: to not let her disability beat her down. She had the medal framed and hung it in the family room where she saw it every day. My mother, now, was running the true marathon.

Oh, yes. One more celebrant was at our dinner after the race. At mile sixteen, another Achilles guide had joined us to run the rest of the way. At the finish line, I had hugged him with far more passion than I'd hugged Ted, and he accompanied me and my parents to dinner. His name is Jim, and I loved and love him with all my heart and soul.

Chapter Ten

Jim and Me

At Sunday brunch after New Year's, 1995, Ardith Eicher and I were catching up. "You know," she said just as we were saying good-bye, "last August, I was working with this consultant, Jim, and I really liked him. Lives in Connecticut. I was wondering if you wanted me to give him your number." Ardith was a vice president of marketing for Clairol.

I hesitated. I preferred to get to know a man (in the classroom, at work, in my building) before I went out with him. So despite Ardith's enthusiasm, I was lukewarm. Still, she had good taste in men—she had been in a relationship with a lovely guy for several years—and I hadn't been going out with anyone for a while. "What's he like?" I asked.

"He's deep," she said immediately, meaning, I supposed, intelligent, reflective. "He's really deep. And cute."

Deep and cute. Not bad. "Sure, give him my number," I said. "But *please* don't say anything about my history to him. If I like him, I want to tell him myself."

"Fine. Anyway, we're not working on the project anymore, so I'm not sure how long it'll take."

The next morning, she called. "Trisha, you won't believe this! I walked into the Clairol building this morning and there's Jim in the lobby. Apparently he's working on another project for Clairol, only this time not with me. I gave him your number. He sounded interested."

The coincidence was intriguing. It had worked out so quickly, so unexpectedly. But then a week went by, and I didn't hear from Jim. Do I call Ardith? I asked myself. Yes, I answered.

"He really did sound like he'd get in touch with you," Ardith assured me, "but if he still hasn't called in another week, call me back." Another week of silence would mean he wasn't interested, I figured. The following Monday was two weeks, and I decided not to bother her again.

When I got home that night, a message was on my machine. "Hi, Trisha. Ardith gave me your number. When you get a chance, give me a call."

Hmmm, I thought. Two weeks! Do I want to call him right back? What's the deal here? And then I figured, Why play games? I called him.

◆

Jim has his own take on our beginnings. "Ardith and I had last seen each other at a business meeting in San Diego," he told me. "It was in August. We were walking together after dinner and all of a sudden she said, 'Would you be interested in meeting any of my single friends in New York City?' I said, 'Sure.' Her next question was 'Well, what kind of woman would you be interested in?' I must have fumbled—how do you answer a question like that? I blurted out, 'Intelligent. Likes the outdoors, adventurous'—like one of those personal ads—and that was the end of it. I didn't hear from her in September, October, November. It's not that I thought about it every day, but I assumed that whatever I said about the kind of woman I'd be interested in just didn't fit any of her friends."

Actually, it did.

The reason he didn't call right away after he'd run into Ardith in the lobby? Because he'd just come back from twenty-one days in Africa, climbing Mt. Kilimanjaro, and had bins of mail waiting for him. His first priority was to catch up. Besides, he didn't see that he was going to be in the city for a while and wasn't ready to commit to a special trip down on the weekend.

Still, he did make that phone call.

◆

I don't remember much about our first conversation, just that I liked the voice at the other end of the line. It all was very casual. Jim didn't say anything about a date or a face-to-face meeting. But he called again, then again and again. Our talks were nice, just getting to know each other. There was a warmth to them, an ease. He made me laugh. And then on one Thursday night he said he was going to be in New York that weekend for a seminar. Shy, proper me jumped in and said, "Well, do you want to get together?"

◆

The seminar was called "Awakening the Healer Within."

Three or four years before, Jim met a woman named Elizabeth Stratton, a spiritual healer and teacher, who was giving a seminar titled "Forgiveness and Letting Go of Judgment." It involved meditation and the laying on of hands as well as good advice, and he found himself responding to a spiritual part in him that he was glad to discover. From time to time, he attended other such seminars. "Awakening the Healer Within" was one of them.

We hadn't discussed Jim's spiritual side in our early phone conversations, but we did that night. He wanted to tell me about this interest in person, he said, because he would be revealing a deeper side of himself and wasn't sure how I'd respond.

On Saturday, he called from a phone booth. The seminar had ended early. Would it be all right if he came up now?

"No!" I yelped into my portable phone. I was still in the bathtub. "Can you give me another hour?"

He rang the downstairs buzzer on time, and through the intercom I told him to get ready for four flights of stairs. I opened the door, stepped into the hallway, and listened for his footsteps. And then there he was, dressed in slacks and a Gore-Tex jacket. He had thinning hair, blue eyes, a wide smile, and the body of an athlete, though he was huffing and puffing from walking up the four flights. Ardith was right: cute.

I was in jeans and a turtleneck, and he seemed as pleased with me as I was with him. "I had to wander around for the last hour," he said, not really complaining. "It's *cold* out there."

I had made a dinner reservation at a neighborhood Italian restaurant, Trattoria de Libertad, which gave us about an hour to sit in my apartment and get to know each other.

How forthcoming he was, how intently he listened to me! He told me about the seminar, about his interest in healing, his desire to open himself to his spiritual side. His words resonated with my own experiences of healing, and his intensity and enthusiasm matched mine. I can't remember being as comfortable with anyone else in so short a time, a comfort I had told Ardith was a prerequisite for revealing my secret. It was a risky moment. Would he be turned off? Repelled? Afraid of the notoriety? Unaccepting?

I hesitated, took a deep breath—and plunged. "I should tell you something. I am the Central Park Jogger."

"I already know," he said solemnly.

My heart lurched. "How?"

"I have a friend who also went to the Yale School of Management and was a summer intern at Salomon. A few days ago, I was talking to her and mentioned the Yale-Salomon connection.

" 'What's her name?' my friend asked.

" 'Trisha Meili.'

" 'Do you know who that is? That's the woman who was attacked in Central Park.' "

It's hard to say precisely how his prior knowledge affected me; *disappointed* is the closest I can come. This was my information, the pivotal part of my life, and it seemed to me unfair that I couldn't control it. I guess it doesn't matter, I told myself. But it *did* matter. I wanted to tell people *after* they knew me, so they wouldn't be affected by preconceived notions of who the Central Park Jogger was.

I shook the feeling off. It wasn't Jim's fault that he knew, and the knowledge didn't seem to make a difference to him. We went to dinner.

❖

It was one of those rare times when a bomb could have exploded beside me and I wouldn't have noticed. I was absorbed in Jim, watching his expressions, listening to his words, enjoying the moment. I sat opposite him at a table next to the wall; a candle between us, its flame reflected in his eyes.

He noticed my eyes too. "You looked beautiful," he told me recently, "but obviously I saw the scar near your eye."

He said he wanted to reach over and touch my face near that scar, a sign of comfort or empathy, but he resisted. That would come later. "You were a person who might have died, a person who even if you had lived had no business sitting beside me having dinner, feeding yourself. So I knew right away you were a survivor." He smiled. "There's a sense of fragility about you, but scratch below the surface a little bit and you'll find somebody who won't be trifled with. I knew right away you were a person who wouldn't break accidentally. You'd been through stuff I doubt I could have made it through. And though I still wanted to touch you and comfort you, I sensed you were stronger than me.

"The first thing I felt from you was your heart, your warmth," Jim explained. "Maybe that's what makes you so strong. Your ability to give your heart to others."

◆

We began seeing each other on weekends, but from that first dinner on, we'd talk on the phone literally every day until we got married. We found out quickly we had shared tastes, especially our love of the outdoors. Before the attack, I'd always enjoyed outside activities, and after it, over the past years, I began to experience nature more deeply, sensing in it the wondrous presence of a mystical power. Jim gave me a greater appreciation of looking and observing. Seeing it through his eyes enhanced my feelings about it too. Our first months together were a wonderful, peaceful time. We weren't doing, doing, doing, but rather we just wanted to be alone together. What we *did* was something marvelous.

We fell in love.

◆

Usually, after I embarked on a relationship, I'd call my parents to tell them about it. This time I called as usual, but hung up feeling I hadn't said enough. I wrote them a long letter telling them about Jim, about the strength of my feelings and the strength of his feelings toward me. My mother wrote back that I'd gone out with other people I'd felt strongly about, but that this time it seemed something had changed. "I'm not quite sure what *makes* him different, but there must be something there," she said. I'm not sure either—it's hard to put words to love. Trust. Support. Lack of constraint. The honesty of our intimate conversations? But they're not nearly enough. *Love* itself will have to do.

◆

Jim and I spoke frequently about the attack and my recovery, but we didn't dwell on them. Like any new couple in love, we were interested in getting to know all aspects of each other, concentrating on what appealed to us the most. Nevertheless, I sometimes wondered how he felt about the effects of my head injury. I was hypersensitive about not being able to keep to my train of thought, or about my attention span wandering or losing my focus or my inability to retrieve words. As a child, I had striven to get everything right and usually succeeded. And here I was, a grown woman, deeply in love, imperfect, "faulty," wondering if Jim wanted to take a long-term risk.

Over time, I became more accepting of myself, but doubts still crept in. At one point, Jim told me he wanted to spend the rest of his life with me. Phew! It wasn't a formal proposal, but it hit hard. This is serious, I thought. Am *I* ready for this kind of commitment? Was he fully aware of my limitations and the difficulties they might bring? Was *I* fully aware of my limitations and the difficulties they might bring?

I don't remember the impetus for the conversation—probably my doubts over whether he would love me with my deficits—but it was before we got married. We were sitting on the couch.

"Are you still going to love me?" I asked. "Do you love me seeing who I am, knowing the things that are wrong with me?"

I remember that Jim hugged me tenderly, then moved a little bit away so he could look into my eyes and let me see his. He said, "I know you're not perfect. Neither am I. It's not like there's a big mystery here and I'm going to suddenly find out about you and say, 'This isn't somebody I want to be with.' I know who you are and I love you for who you are and you don't have to be afraid I'm going to leave you because of something I find out."

It was a tremendous moment.

And now—though not always—I can joke about it. "Give me a break, I've got a brain injury," I'll say if someone asks too tough a question or assigns too difficult a job. But at times when my brain gets tired, it's disappointing and humiliating and anything but a joke. Sometimes I'm able to say, "You know what? It doesn't matter." Sometimes I find myself saying, "Oh, I forgot this," or, "I didn't think this through." I think it's the result of the head injury, but I still get mad at myself. I don't like being frustrated.

◆

We had gotten to a point of wanting to spend the rest of our lives together. But we each resisted the convention of marriage. The need to "license" our commitment seemed unnecessary; it wouldn't change the depth of our feelings and level of trust. Thus, having a marriage blessed by the church (Jim's Presbyterian, I'm Catholic) or legalized by the state of Connecticut felt redundant. What difference would a ceremony make? I even told Jim I didn't want an engagement ring since only women wore one and it seemed an anachronistic symbol of possession— my Wellesley spirit coming through.

A year after we met, I took Jim to the Rainbow Room for his birthday, as glamorous a place as there is in New York City. It was February 2. We were all dressed up. "Do you want to dance?" Jim asked toward the end of our meal. We walked down from our table to the large, circular dance floor in the middle of the restaurant. Jim took me in his arms. The band was playing. I was relieved the music was slow because my balance problems made it necessary to hold on. Jim had maneuvered us to the very center of the room.

"Oh, we're right in the middle of the floor," I said, somewhat surprised.

"What would you say if I asked you to marry me?"

A thunderbolt. I remembered a time, some eight months before, when I was visiting Jim for the weekend, and we had a romantic lobster dinner and, as Jim put it, "more margaritas than we probably should have." We were standing at the sink doing the dishes when I asked him virtually the same question: "What would you say if I asked you to marry me right now?" His answer was simple: "You had too many margaritas." And that was that.

But now, without margaritas, in the middle of the floor of the Rainbow Room, *he* asked *me*.

"Ask me the right way and find out," I said.

"Will you marry me?"

"Yes."

So what had changed?

"I just have these feelings," he told me. "I'm proud of our relationship and feel so good about it I want to go public."

The man got off without having to buy me an engagement ring.

Marriage means giving up a measure of independence, I knew, the very freedom I had striven for during my adolescence and college years and fought so passionately to regain after the attack. Even with Jim, I keep fighting for it. I don't want to become too dependent on him.

Part of Jim's nature is to always want to help me with things I'm doing—set up a new computer, say, or carry a kayak up from the beach—but often my first reaction is to want to do it myself. A part of me still needs to push and test my abilities. Even when trying to recall a word or a name, I'll say, "Wait, wait, don't tell me. I want to figure this out for myself." It's just like exercising my muscles. The more I work on my brain, the more it will respond.

Once we bought new equipment for my office, which is on the third floor of our house. That meant carrying down the old equipment to the basement for storage—heavy equipment that even Jim would have difficulty handling. He told me he'd do it when he returned from a meeting he had that day, but by the time he got home, I'd moved it.

Jim put it best: "Part of you says, 'Yeah, I'd love to have this white knight on a horse come and slay all my dragons and take me away to the castle,' and that's in conflict with 'but I want to be my own person.' It's kind of searching for the balance between being cared for and at the same time not being smothered."

Still, when he proposed, my "Yes" was heartfelt; I'd worked the independence/reliance issue through in my mind. I was comfortable getting married because I felt our marriage would provide an environment that would allow me to develop more.

On Mother's Day, 1996, he said, "Well, *when* do you want to get married?"

Our nature-loving spirits wanted an outdoor wedding. "Maybe spring of next year," I answered.

"How about September?"
"Of this year?"
"Yeah."

I was breathing hard. "Let's see if we can pull it together," I thought.

We called our overjoyed parents to tell them of our plans.

◆

A hurricane worked its way up the East Coast the week of our wedding, providing some worrisome moments. But it turned out to have no significance, actually or metaphorically: September 15, 1996, was sunny and mild, and we've had no damaging storms in our marriage.

The ceremony was held in a beach club on Long Island Sound. We would say our vows standing in the sunshine just a few steps from the beach. The sound of the small waves breaking on the sand provided a peaceful background. My best friend, Jane, was my maid of honor.

A Unitarian minister presided. Bob Herber, who with his wife, Peggy, had shown us so much love, read from *The Prophet* by Kahlil Gibran; Jim's sister Jayne read from Anne Morrow Lindbergh's *Gift from the Sea.* Jim and I had written our own service, our own vows:

> *I, Trisha, take you, Jim, as my husband, loving what I know of you, trusting what I don't yet know. As we face into the uncertainty of our future together, with both the joys and adversities of being a couple in love, I commit to honor your goals and dreams, to be mindful of your needs and clear*

*about my own, to have the courage to grow, to laugh and
have a sense of humor, for all our days together.*

We exchanged rings. We were introduced as husband and
wife. We kissed. The ceremony was over. Flooded with joy and
appreciation, I turned to face our guests, many of whom had
supported me through the difficult years. There were Pat Garrett, who had identified my battered body in the hospital; Ken,
who had come to sit at my bedside and helped with my care;
Tom Strauss, who symbolized all that Salomon had done for me
and my family; Lisa Borowitz, my protector and communicator
when I was unable to communicate myself; Liz and Bob from
Select Fitness, who had pushed me to regain my strength; Pat
Dunlavy, whose confidence in me had helped me believe in
myself; Ted Rogers, my Achilles guide who had gotten me
through the New York City Marathon; Ardith, our matchmaker
and my stalwart friend. And of course my own family, who had
suffered through the uncertainty of my recovery with unconditional love and unwavering support.

For Pat Garrett, whose feelings may have reflected what many
others felt, the wedding brought back troubling memories: identifying me, watching me struggle through the first days, seeing me
slowly recover at Salomon. "The wedding signified you were back
to normal," he told me later. "Healthy, getting on with your life,
married, walking off into the sunset on the beach."

It was actually 4 P.M. and the sun was still high. But it seems
everybody remembers us walking hand in hand into the sunset,
and if the fantasy of it pleases them, it also pleases me. A sunset
wouldn't have made the ceremony any more romantic.

Chapter Eleven

The Man in the Wheelchair

The Easter Sunday after we were married, Jim and I went hiking in a forest some distance from our house, and I remember saying that I wanted to do something else with my life. I wasn't really complaining to him about work, but rather envisioning a time when I could use my experience positively, though I still wasn't sure how. I talked about the mind/body connection and how exciting the concept was. About recovery. About the effect all the support I'd received had had on my healing. About making a difference. About—

Jim stopped walking and looked at me. "You know what? Whenever you talk about this, your eyes light up. Your whole *face* lights up. Your expression changes. *This* is what excites you."

Neither of us was certain precisely what "this" meant, but clearly it involved doing something that helped people in some way, and I said so. He was immediately supportive. "If it means leaving Salomon, so be it."

I've always taken my time before acting—and maybe post-attack the tendency's grown stronger. I think about the various options, consider pros and cons, try to look into the future to predict the repercussions. I knew that if I left Salomon, I'd be giving up a good salary, the support of my colleagues, the comfort of the familiar.

The first didn't overly bother me. Loss of my salary might mean giving up certain luxuries, but we've always lived simply: we have an unpretentious house and wanted nothing more elaborate. We enjoy eating at home and have no kids to put through college. If our decision meant changing our lifestyle, that would be okay.

Giving up safety was more difficult. My boss, my friends at work, the energy of my days, and the familiarity of my environment were, as I've noted, vital factors in my recovery. *That* was a lot to give up. I needed to think about it.

◆

In the fall of 1997, Travelers Group announced its merger with Salomon, though everyone knew the company had acquired us; it would not actively take over our management for a few months. As in every such takeover we were all trying to find our comfort levels, wondering what the change would mean, being evasive about plans, trying to decide whether to stay—but the merger prompted me to finally make my decision. I would leave, not to go to a different investment bank, but to try something new. The whispers in my head quieted down.

I told my boss, Pat Dunlavy, a few weeks later. He understood my desire to leave, but asked me to stay on until the spring to help ease the transition. I agreed. Before that day, I had never job-hunted, networked, or explored other avenues of work while I was at Salomon. Now, however, with my departure date set, I began to look around.

Look for what? Something directly related to my recovery? I was afraid of what such a move represented psychologically. I knew I'd be working with a whole new set of people; did I also want to do something that would potentially remind me every single day of what had happened that night in Central Park? I'd been on the board at SAVI and was currently on the boards of Achilles and Gaylord, but that was different from working directly with rape survivors or the disabled. Something in an allied field, I thought, might serve my needs—a nonprofit service agency, a foundation.

Before leaving the security of the place I had known, the people who had been with me through so much, I decided to explore the corporate giving arm of Travelers, which had an established foundation funding nonprofit service agencies and other philanthropic causes. Perhaps there were opportunities there. The people I met with were cordial and helped educate me on foundation work, but it didn't feel comfortable. I'd be working with Travelers people, not my comrades, and I knew in my heart that though part of me wanted to cling to the old Salomon, no matter how changed, I had to step out more, indeed get away entirely. Still, foundation work seemed promising.

So there I was—no income, no daily schedule or routine. I sensed the answer to my quest wouldn't come tap me on the shoulder; I would have to work hard at my search. It meant eighteen months of introspection and exploration. I met with executive recruiters, spoke with foundations and nonprofits and volunteered weekly at the rehabilitation center in my town. Eventually, something clicked.

The Achilles Track Club received some of its support from an organization called The Clark Foundation, so I arranged to talk to its executive director. "One organization we're funding does remarkable work," he told me. "It's called The Bridge Fund. They help the working poor who are threatened with losing their housing. Indeed, their mission is to *prevent* people from becoming homeless. If you're interested, I'll set up a meeting for you with Oscar, the man who, with his wife, started it."

Interested? Very.

Oscar Pollock, in his sixties, was energetic and full of enthusiasm. I liked him from the first. He explained that social service agencies and religious organizations referred to The Bridge Fund those who, because of some emergency—sudden medical problems, the death of the breadwinner, the loss of a job—might be unable to pay their rent and faced eviction. These were the working poor, ineligible for government assistance unless they got a lot poorer. The organization's purpose was to give them interest-free loans, thus providing a "bridge" until their situation improved. To help them avoid the downward spiral of homelessness, it also provided budget counseling and advice on maneuvering through the bureaucratic intricacies of the housing court system in New York City and Westchester County.

The Bridge Fund started in Westchester in the late 1980s, he explained, then opened offices in Manhattan, Brooklyn, and the Bronx. Oscar had grown tired of his ever more taxing role as overseer, and besides, he also had a full-time job. He needed someone to step in for him and do the day-to-day running of the organization. Did I think I could be that person?

I wouldn't be working with rape survivors or people with TBI at The Bridge Fund, so I wouldn't be confronted daily with my history—I didn't think I could handle that yet. But I *would* be serving those in need. I told him my history and he felt that experience gave me a sensitivity that would be an asset to the organization. I pointed out that I had little managerial experience at Salomon; Oscar didn't think this was a problem. So it seemed a wonderful opportunity to step into the nonprofit world. I would, I imagined, have time for hands-on work with the organization's clients. I would develop managerial skills. My salary, while not what I had made at Salomon, was adequate. And most important, The Bridge Fund offered hope and possibility to people so that their lives would go on as they overcame the blocks in their paths. Perfect.

I had never before held a position of such responsibility, and I was in an entirely new situation. It was my first job away from the protected environment of Salomon. Here there was no such protection. Three people reported to me directly, including the executive directors of the New York City and Westchester offices (I usually worked part of the week in Manhattan, part in Westchester), and I was nervous. What would it do to me psychologically? How would my brain injury affect my performance?

Almost at once, I ran into difficulties. Not surprisingly, as president I was pulled in many different directions: supervising fund-raising; planning events; overseeing financial reporting and budgeting; managing the staff; and working with the board of directors. I began to feel overwhelmed. In my lowest, most frustrating moments, and there were many, I felt I wasn't doing my job well, and I constantly graded myself against an ideal I had mentally established—an old pattern, of course. Too often I failed. My inner critic reappeared with a vengeance.

Life is exhausting when everything is a test, and at The Bridge Fund the tests kept coming. Competing against myself was dangerous; when I played by my self-imposed rules, I could never win, never be satisfied. Night after night I came home and complained to Jim. I couldn't handle it, I told him. My injury made me unfit for the job. It was too much, no fun. I felt depleted, anxious. It made my head ache. Issues I had worked through with Dr. Kleiman resurfaced. Jim was solicitous, unfailingly kind, but I think my grousing got on his nerves.

I saw that the staff felt passionate about their work, and together we accomplished an expansion of our services and exceeded our fund-raising goals—by objective standards I probably passed the tests I thought I'd failed. But I knew that my dedication couldn't match theirs and more and more realized that what I needed was work directly related to the core experience of my life. By the end of a year I was pretty sure I'd leave The Bridge Fund. In my typical fashion, I waited another six months before resigning.

May 2001. Again, no job, no income, no daily schedule or routine. Yet with Jim's support, I never panicked. When I had talked to him during that hike some four years earlier, I had felt a passion for sharing the importance of support. If it was my conviction that the spiritual is as vital to healing as traditional Western medicine—if *that's* what excited and animated me—then I'd find meaningful work where my voice could proclaim it. I'd have to become "more public," though, and I was still apprehensive.

I began slowly, even while I was at The Bridge Fund, by giving a talk at a Brain Injury Association Conference in Washington, D.C., about the results of the research project I had worked on with Dr. Gordon supporting the benefits of exercise for TBI survivors. I didn't talk as "the Central Park Jogger," but rather as someone who had suffered a traumatic brain injury and who strongly believed that exercise had played an important role in her recovery.

Soon after, Iona Siegel, director of SAVI, asked me if I would speak to a group of SAVI trainees about the importance of the organization's work.

"Your perspective will be especially helpful," she said. "You weren't in any condition to even be aware of us—you were in a coma—but I believe SAVI was of great help to your family. As co-survivors they needed to keep focus on you, not be distracted by the press or the racial controversy. We helped them do that."

Iona's request intrigued me. But was I the appropriate person to speak to the trainees? I had never really identified myself strongly with being a rape survivor, for though I'd certainly been raped, I had no memory of it, no symptoms of PTSD such as nightmares or flashbacks. I couldn't describe the psychological aftereffects of a rape. But I had daily, painful issues with my head injury. When I worked with others who had the same disability, our empathy was immediate and powerful. Wouldn't it be better if I spoke to them? When I broached my doubts to Iona, she assured me that other rape survivors and those who worked with them would gain strength from me.

Each year, there are about one hundred new SAVI volunteers or advocates—those who are called to emergency rooms to give counseling to sexual assault and domestic violence survivors and their families—and they go through a forty-hour training program held over a couple of months. So I would be speaking to a large audience, I knew, yet it would be on a subject that went to the depth of my being: the role others had played in my recovery. And it was a safe environment. My personal story, and the part SAVI had played in it, might inspire the trainees, some of whom were rape survivors themselves. I could show them how important their work is in helping others like me. I said yes to Iona. I now believed I could talk to an audience both as Trisha Meili and the Central Park Jogger and my world would not tilt off its axis.

For the first time I had exposed my experience to an audience. I felt comfortable, though, and exhilarated by the positive feedback. I still wasn't sure just how much I would reveal, just how public I wanted to be. But I began to see a connection between my experience and my potential future work.

◆

The slender, tousle-haired man with intense eyes and a runner's build was teaching us to eat a raisin. Not by biting it and swallowing it as most people do, he said, but by eating it *"mindfully, with awareness."* About forty of us were in a session at an April 1997 conference, "Healing the Whole Self," sponsored by the Omega Institute, and each of us, following his instructions, looked at our raisin, smelled it, brought it gradually to our mouth—experiencing the flow of saliva our actions induced—and at last savored it. Fabulous! Never in my life had I tasted a raisin so *consciously.*

The teacher was Jon Kabat-Zinn, and his class was not on culinary arts, but was titled "Using the Power of Your Body and Mind to Face Stress." Jon was founder and director of the Stress Reduction Clinic at the University of Massachusetts Medical Center. At the core of his philosophy lies the concept of *mindfulness*, which, paraphrasing his definition, is about paying attention in the present moment, about waking up and living in harmony with oneself and the rest of the world. About cultivating some appreciation for the fullness of each moment we are alive. About not dwelling in the past or wishing for the future.

In other words, about *exactly what I was doing at Gaylord.* It was an amazing epiphany. As a result of my injuries, I found that I was constantly paying attention to what my mind and body were doing. I had to, because nothing came naturally—I was in the midst of relearning. Remaining in the present, focusing on the task directly in front of me, using my mind to stay aware of what my body was doing, concentrating on what was happening *now*, were, I'm convinced, precisely the tools that speeded my rehabilitation. I had not been consumed with what was or what might have been. I was mindful, living in the present, using the power of my body and mind.

Soon after this conference, I read Jon's book on mindfulness called *Wherever You Go, There You Are* and recognized that he, among other things, expressed with wonderful clarity ideas on the mind/body connection and its effects on healing that I had been trying to articulate for years. I had expressed to Jim my wish for a philosophical mentor. Jon's message was clear and powerful, and his credentials in the medical community substantiated the ideas I was beginning to voice. I felt a powerful connection to him. Dare I approach him? I wondered.

I'm naturally reticent and it took me until August 1998 to work up enough nerve, but finally I wrote him. I admit I used my "media" name, quite shamelessly figuring I had a better chance for a response if he knew who I was.

> I also believe in a mind/body connection to healing after my recovery from a serious, life-threatening event. I am the person who was beaten and raped while running in Central Park nine years ago—the person the press called "the Central Park Jogger."
>
> A few months ago I left my job on Wall Street to take some time to listen to what my heart is calling me to do. I have always had a fascination with the body—what it can do and become. This fascination became so much more personal as I witnessed my own body transform from a person sitting in a wheelchair unable to remember the events from a novel's previous page to someone who helped manage a bond trading floor and ran the New York City Marathon in 4½ hours!
>
> I would like to be able to use my firsthand experience of recovery to help others who are in a healing process. At this point in my search, I am not sure where best to focus my efforts.

*To continue to educate myself about this field, I am
attending the Body and Soul conference in Boston in
September at which you are speaking. I would be honored to
speak with you in greater depth about what areas, given my
background, interests and experience, I might explore in the
field of the mind/body connection to health and healing.*

He called back almost immediately and told me he'd be glad to
see me in Boston. When we met, he was welcoming, supportive,
and friendly, but had no specific career advice. It was, as always,
an inspiration to hear him speak, but there was no profound
communication between us.

Nevertheless, a year later, when I got my job at The Bridge
Fund, I wrote to thank him for his help, as I did everyone in the
network who had assisted me during my job exploration. This
time he wrote back—and his response was remarkable:

*The Bridge Fund is obviously a worthy organization, and it
is also obvious that the appointment is a testimony to the
huge work on yourself that you have been doing over the
years. . . .*

*Not even knowing anything of the details of your challenges
and struggles, I intuit that your rehabilitation reflects a
profound tenacity and faith in yourself and in life. I have been
giving talks to professional rehab audiences of late, and make
the point that the deep meaning of the word* rehabilitation *is
"to live inside again" (as in the French* habiter—*to dwell, to
inhabit). So rehabilitation is the learning to live inside not only
one's body, however it is after an injury or illness, but inside
one's very being. And that often takes, in the face of huge*

hurdles, a powerful intentionality and discipline. That is what
the inner/outer work of mindfulness is about. Clearly, in your
own way, you embody it and bring it to life.

Not only had he put into words my own thoughts, he gave
me an idea that, without his letter, I would never have followed
up. I wrote him back on December 20.

I was excited to hear you are speaking to professional rehab
audiences. Your point about the need "to live inside again" is
absolutely right! Regardless of your injury, your life is
changed and is different. As I have learned, "different" does
not necessarily mean "worse." But lots of hard, painful work
is needed to reflect, "go deep," and, in time, be thankful for
all that your body has done for you to get where you are. As
you so well know, this hard work results in a wonderful
richness.

    I suppose what excited me most is that you are giving this
message to those who can help make it happen. Obviously,
the rehab professionals cannot make the process happen for
the patient. But, if they have an appreciation for the process,
they can be supportive of the patient during the time of "living
inside again." I am a true believer in the healing benefits of
support. I know it was crucial to my recovery!

    . . . When I look back on my rehabilitation process with
this new awareness of mindfulness, I see something that
surprises me. It appears that my consciousness instinctively
knew what to do to help me heal. I can see evidence of my
mindfulness and my "living inside" that you mentioned, yet I
had no exposure to these concepts. I do not understand why,

but I believe that something in me responded to my
rehabilitation in a mindful way. I did not reflect on the past
and say "why?" or worry about what I would or would not
be able to do in the future. Instead, I worked in the present to
make my reality as good as it could be. Obviously, I am so
very grateful that an inner wisdom took hold.

If you ever speak in the Connecticut/New York area
please let me know. I would love to listen to you. Also, if I
may be so bold, I would enjoy delivering the message with
you from the patient's perspective. Let me know what you
think.

Mine was an offer to step from privacy into the public eye, and
it's difficult to convey now the fear and excitement I felt as I
made it. *This* was my act of courage. I offered to reveal myself to
an audience of strangers. If I *really* wanted to give a message of
hope and possibility to others, this was the place to start. I
waited anxiously for Jon's response. It came in an e-mail:

Thank you for your wonderful letter. . . . Yes, it certainly
sounds as if you came to mindfulness on your own, and that
is even more wonderful than hearing about it first. But it is
extraordinary, especially in light of what occurred, that you
somehow knew to focus on the present rather than be caught
up in what was already over, even though it had happened
and was so horrible.

I am glad that from your experience, the orientation of
learning to "live inside again" is fundamental to rehabilitation
and to healing. I love the idea of perhaps delivering such a
message together, so I thank you for being so "bold." The

*venues in which I have delivered this particular message so
far have been conferences put on by Harvard Medical School
and the Spaulding Rehab Hospital on Complementary and
Alternate Approaches in Rehabilitation Medicine. They take
place in Boston, not in New York City. The next one will be
next fall, perhaps October 19–20, 2000. . . . What would
you think of giving a presentation together at such a
conference? . . . That is, if you wouldn't mind coming to
Boston.*

"I love the idea of perhaps delivering such a message
together," he'd written. I couldn't believe it! Yes, I had asked, but
I hadn't really expected such a warmhearted response. He wants
to deliver a message *together,* I repeated to myself, a message I've
been developing for years. He's literally helping me find my
voice. Chills ran through my body. I ran to show Jim the letter.

Later, Jon told me that before he met me, he had been moved
by my story as many others had, experiencing the "spasm of
empathy" that had seized the country. Now that he knew me, he
said, it was my tenacity, my will to heal and move on by working in the present moment to recover the depth of my being,
that impressed him. I wear his finding those things in me like a
badge of honor.

What a difference from my old preoccupation with deficits!

My kinship with him, with his ideas, exciting as it was at the
time, now seems preordained. Without my knowing it then, our
joint appearance would be one of those rare times when life
turns around and you start off on a path you knew existed but
could not find the right map to point you to it. Jon provided the
map. A man in a wheelchair was to locate the direction.

Actually, our presentation was not held until May 14, 2001, as part of Spaulding Rehabilitation Hospital's Distinguished Speakers series. Before it, Jon and I corresponded regularly and met once for lunch in New York City. In the fall of 2000 I wrote him a long letter that outlined what I had been thinking, the message I wanted to convey to the audience at Spaulding. Putting words to these feelings was difficult for me and took longer than I thought it would—maybe this was because of my brain injury, though such ideas would be difficult to define precisely, I suppose, for anyone. I wanted to get them right and say them clearly. They are my core beliefs about recovery and healing, the "voice" Jon helped me find.

. . . In terms of my potential contribution to a joint endeavor, I am not an expert on mindfulness and the mind/body connection to healing. Yet I can contribute personal anecdotes that can support each.

Perhaps what I believe in most strongly is the mystery of life and its ability to heal. More specifically, here are some examples of what my experience has given me.

The power of intention.

I have read about the number of people around the world praying for me while I lay in the hospital, a woman they knew only as "the Central Park Jogger." Those prayers made a difference. I received letters from many strangers who sent their thoughts and prayers, and even now, when I meet people and I share my history with them, many say,

"I prayed for you." I believe that so many focused on my recovery, through thoughts, prayers and intentions, were an instrumental healing factor.

The power of the body.

I believe our body knows how to heal without our conscious intervention (similar to a scab forming after a cut). It knows to operate in the present moment! I dealt with the present moment—before I was conscious of its importance and impact—because that was all I could control. I just concentrated on me and on healing and I don't remember worrying about things I could not control—like the justice system. I focused on the reality that was mine and the physical, emotional and psychological aspects of my injury began to improve. . . .

The power of touch.

During my early days in Metropolitan Hospital, while still in a coma, I was connected to many tubes. I'm told I would sometimes thrash around and the hospital was concerned that I would disconnect machines that were keeping me alive. To prevent this, I was sometimes tied to the bed when not enough staff were available to watch me. A private nurse was brought in and she has told me she would often hold me and comfort me when I became agitated. This calmed me down. It was not a widely accepted practice at the hospital, but a psychiatrist saw her one day and commented, "Good. I am glad you are doing that." She also brought relaxation tapes and played them for me in the hospital room.

The power of support.

Unconditional love and support came from so many sources. I have formed strong friendships with people I didn't know before the attack. They wrote to me continuously and a level of trust was formed between us in spite of us being strangers. In fact, one read at my wedding. These bonds contributed to my healing.

The power of the mind.

After I began to run again, I assumed I no longer had the stamina to run a marathon—and that was OK. Several years later, I saw I was stronger than I thought and *wanted* to experience a New York City Marathon. The physical part of me said, "Your knees and body can't take it," but my mind kept pushing me and I *was* able to run 26 miles, crossing the finish line in 4½ hours, a very average time! Now, my mind doesn't have the desire. So, I'm not registering for any more marathons!

The power of no resentment.

I believe that not harboring any resentment toward whoever attacked me made a huge difference to my healing. Yes, I did feel anger. Yes, I wanted justice and participated in the process. But, I was able to focus much of my energy on healing and did not let the anger and resentment eat away at me and prevent me from progressing.

The power of doing.

Many times I challenged myself, taking risks, pushing to try new things. I still listened to my body, but being in these "unprotected" situations, while being very aware of my limitations, forced me to adjust and adapt to circumstances. For example, my balance was affected by the head injury. Accepting a job on the Salomon trading floor with its crowded, narrow passageways was a test to my maneuverability. I was mindful of how and where I walked and I found I was able to get around with little trouble.

My experience has also given me a desire to express to people that each one of us has the ability to make a difference in the life of someone else—to help make a miracle happen. So many helped my miracle happen in so many ways!

As it turned out, my speech at Spaulding was more personal and less organized than the thoughts I wrote down for Jon. But the ideas lay behind everything I said that day, just as they lie behind this book. I insisted on not making my fame the focal point of my appearance—I wanted the audience to hear what I had to say, not gawk at the Jogger. Even the posters announcing the event simply read Trisha Meili and identified me as a "TBI survivor," and of course Jon's name was prominent. The title of our presentation, "The Power of the Human Heart: A Story of Trauma & Recovery and Its Implications for Rehabilitation and Healing," might have been a bit daunting, but it got across the idea.

Our audience of about seventy was composed of clinicians and current and former patients with brain injuries and their families. I introduced myself briefly as the Central Park Jogger— my first time saying this before a general audience—then Jon spoke both about me and about learning to live inside again. He

led us in a meditation exercise, ringing bells to bring us to awareness of our bodies and our breathing, and when I spoke, I did so
calmly and without nervousness. (That Jim was there helped.) I
described the difficulty of my physical and mental rehabilitation, emphasizing that living in the present and accepting my
condition in that present helped my recovery dramatically. I said
that learning to live inside again is not an easy process, that it
requires patience to endure the inevitable frustrations of a slow
recovery, a body that can't always do what it used to do. And I
talked about hope and possibility.

I ended my formal remarks with words coming as much from
my heart as my brain:

> None of us, injured or not, are the same as we were even
> yesterday. Because of what I saw happen to me naturally, I
> am such a strong believer in working in the present and
> making whatever reality you have as positive and produc-
> tive and healthy as it can be. It works. And I'd like each of
> you here to remember that you all are part of the healing
> process. I encourage you to use your heart as you engage in
> that healing process. On behalf of former and current and
> future patients, I enthusiastically thank you for what each
> of you does.

The response was all I had hoped for. It was obvious that people
were moved, that Jon and I were helpful. But nothing meant as
much to me as the time after our prepared comments—the time
of questions and answers.

A clinician asked when I became aware of the benefits of
mindfulness. The husband of a woman with a brain tumor asked

about both the physical and mental aspects to healing. Another clinician, noting that many people—family members as well as sufferers—wanted to know about the future, wondered how best to get patients to stay in the present. One patient spoke about her feeling of loss of self and the struggle it took to regain it; another, saying her body felt like an unsafe place, talked about her fear of going inside herself. I asked her to make the distinction between feeling unsafe and feeling different, something I myself had felt most deeply. Jon and I answered them all, he from his experience and I from mine.

In the back row was a man sitting in a wheelchair, an outpatient who had been staring at us throughout the session. Now he raised his hand—the last of the audience to speak. His words were directed at me.

"I'd like to say that you are an inspiration to me. I was in a coma for three and a half months, I couldn't talk for over a year, and I'm in a wheelchair and will walk just like you. Being here has been one of the greatest days of my life. You're so inspirational to me, the most inspirational person I've ever met."

I felt tears come to my eyes. Though we were many feet apart, I felt a closeness with him that can only be described as mystical. I took a few steps toward him. "Thank you so much," I said, "but I want you to look at yourself too and be proud of yourself. You said you were in a coma for three and a half months and you couldn't talk—and look at what you can do now."

"You used to be in a wheelchair?" he asked.

"Yes."

"You give me great hope. It can be done. I can beat this."

A perfect stranger, yet he has been with me ever since. As I inspired him, so he has inspired me.

◆

My work with Jon Kabat-Zinn, the strength of my marriage to Jim, and my belief that I had at last found the road I would follow gave me courage to face the question that I had run from at Salomon and The Bridge Fund: How bad was the damage the attack had wrought? *I need to quiet doubt and face the unknown,* I knew.

I made an appointment at Gaylord for another neurological evaluation.

The results showed nothing dramatic, nor did I expect to find out anything dire. And, also as I suspected, I had made gains in such areas as attention span, recall, and cognitive ability in the intervening years. But it will always take me longer to process information than I once could; I don't pick up on complicated narratives quickly—even *The West Wing* can be hard for me to follow; when too much is going on, my ability to concentrate and prioritize is affected. *Mentally, I will never be the same as I was before the attack.*

To acknowledge this to myself is, to say the least, not a great feeling, though in another way, it gives me peace. I accept it. I can live with it. It is a giant step in my healing. It is part of the woman I've become, and most days I like that woman.

◆

When Jon Kabat-Zinn asked me to appear with him at Spaulding, I called my parents to tell them of the honor. They did not know who he was, so I sent them some material on his work, wanting them to understand why I was so excited. My mother, to whom

I had described my thoughts as they developed, had always been hesitant about my "going public." She was afraid of the impact on me and was also concerned for my physical safety. I assured her that the audience would be sympathetic and that I'd be fine.

Shortly after the talk, I described it to my mom. I didn't expect her to subscribe to the power of mindfulness in healing, but I wanted her to understand my dedication to this philosophy. I told her how I believed I had inspired the man in the wheelchair. How he had inspired me, and how I longed to pass it to others. She was excited for me—I could hear it in her voice: "Maybe this will lead you to what you want to do."

It was the last conversation I had with her before she unexpectedly died in her sleep a few days later.

The shock took time to sink in. She was the rock of my youth, the most valiant warrior on my behalf, my moral conscience. I miss her sorely. I had just written her about visiting for her birthday in July so that I could share in person my excitement over where my journey was heading. That letter arrived the day she died. She never saw it.

Her final words to me resounded in my head. She understood that I was searching for a way to express my passion, that I was responding to a "calling," and that she approved was of great comfort. I felt she understood me and that she had given me permission to proceed.

My steps had led to this, I realized: I could make a difference in the lives of others, just as others had made a difference in my recovery. I am a woman who has been inspired by the capacity of the human spirit to be well. Now I wanted to reach other peoples' spirits, other peoples' hearts.

I started my book.

Epilogue

Events, people, and conditions came together to help me heal. I was not defeated by what happened. That healing continues and will, I hope, for the rest of my life. There is no end to it and that is the beauty of the process—the learning and growing never stop. I've learned that healing is as much a function of the heart as it is of medicine. That in recovery one must push and push to get better, yet balance that drive against a recognition of limits that must be realistically accepted. That you will be amazed by achieving what you and others thought you could never achieve. That it's better to be proud of how far you've come than regret the distance—sometimes unreachable—yet to travel. That care for others generates care in yourself. That when you are your most vulnerable, a relationship of trust with caregivers makes all the difference. That pouring your energy into the present rather than being preoccupied with the past is crucial. That the human spirit is majestic in its ability to comfort and be comforted.

Some early writings on my case reflected that I hadn't yet "reached my peak" and now probably never would. That "I could have been or done so much more." That kind of thinking saddens me. What I've learned over the past fourteen years is that it doesn't matter what I *could* have been. What matters is who I *am* right now.

And that is a survivor named Trisha Meili who may still not be able to walk steadily or see without double vision or be able to juggle too many ideas at once in her mind. But I have the capacity to be generous and to love. Rather than take away these attributes, the attack allowed me to find them in myself.

For that I am grateful.

Afterword

In the months since my book was published, the confirming, encouraging, sympathetic responses have lifted me up, just as they did after the attack itself. I feel buoyed by the knowledge that my story gave others hope. It was what I had set out to do.

A few of the messages surprised me. Some expected me to have a stronger reaction to Matias Reyes's statement that he and he alone attacked me, and that DNA evidence bore out at least the first part of his statement. I didn't. Why, I wondered, is my lack of intense feelings different from their expectations? Is my reaction "wrong"? Am I suppressing or denying my emotions? Can I not handle this contradictory news? Or am I simply applying lessons—focusing on the moment and putting my energy into moving forward—learned along my road to recovery?

I realize that my immediate reaction to Reyes's claim was much like my reaction to the news of the nature of the attack that Assistant District Attorney Elizabeth Lederer brought me at Gaylord Hospital fourteen years ago. Then I was initially stunned and unable to deal with the implications. But instinctively, I changed my focus to where I was and what I had to do to get better. When Reyes confessed, I didn't need to put all my energy into my healing as I had then, but I had a new task to concentrate on: the writing of my book. Now, however, my recovery was continuing smoothly and the book was finished.

I determined to look more deeply into why my reaction to Reyes differed from others' expectations.

◆

The initial question was simple: From the distance of fourteen years, and with support and counseling, I've been dealing psychologically with being brutally beaten, raped, and left for dead. I'd accepted that six men were my assailants—the five young men convicted of the crime and the "other" whose semen stained my sock. Without memory of the horrific event, I had no emotional response to them as individuals. Should the possibility that it was only one man induce a strong reaction at all? And if so, *what* reaction? Relief? Horror? I felt neither. Whether Reyes was only one or one of several who raped me didn't change the fact of the attack or the extent of my injuries. Why should it matter how many were involved?

Yet Reyes was a *fact*, a new element. I tried to analyze my response to a man who, without question, had raped and almost killed me—whether he acted alone or not—and was eager to talk about what he had done. Did I want to study that face and listen as from Reyes's mouth came details of his vicious predatory behavior ("I took a tree branch and hit her with it, then dragged . . .")? Reyes was part of my life—had, if one believes him, single-handedly changed it forever. Shouldn't I look at him squarely, if only from a distance? There was an ABC television show devoted entirely to Reyes and his claim from prison. I hadn't watched it when it was aired. Did I want to watch it now?

I was conflicted. On one side was, "What's the benefit—what would I gain by listening to Reyes? I'm happy. Able to own up to my frailties and accept them. I live and deal with the effects of what was done to me every day—that is my reality. Why should I subject myself to more of his violence through his actions or words?" There was a chance that his face and his words would become part of my consciousness, and I didn't want that. If I heard his voice, saw him move, watched his facial expressions and body language, would I be thinking about him all the time? Might I get hooked by those images?

Though I remained sure that the sight of Reyes wouldn't bring up flashbacks, I did not want to focus on him. Even the glimpses of Reyes in the paper and on the TV news I had allowed myself made me shudder, just as I still shudder when I see the videotaped confessions of the five originally accused young men. While I told myself not to think about Reyes, every once in a while he crept into the corners of my consciousness. It made little sense to expose myself to him any more than I had. I'd worked hard to transform myself from a victim to a survivor and did not want to allow Reyes to make me relinquish the strength that comes from this perspective, to cause me to carry around my victimhood in my head.

On the other hand, many claim that for therapeutic reasons it is essential to look at the causes of trauma directly—confront them—in order to assist healing. Was I avoiding Reyes out of cowardice? Was I constructing a defense against feelings I was unwilling to confront? I had testified at the trial of my five alleged attackers and I had returned to the site of the assault—so I knew I wasn't a coward. As for constructing a protective defense of detachment: well, perhaps. I seem to have done that. Yet I still get mad at trivial indignities, like a person cutting me off in traffic or someone next to me on a train talking loudly on a cell phone. Why I can stay detached from the large and react to the small will have to await further analysis. I suppose, to some extent, it's human nature.

In the end, I decided not to watch the television show. Reyes's words would be more chilling, I thought, than the pictures of him I saw in the papers. The night of April 19, 1989, I couldn't escape his depravity, but now I can, and choose to. It isn't a final decision; I have a tape of the ABC program and someday may play it. I'm still in the process of healing, and maybe I'll change my mind and decide it might indeed serve as another step in the journey.

◆

Other feelings arose in me from Reyes's statement that the five accused of attacking me had not been involved. I am confused. In turmoil. Arguments on both sides seem plausible. The New York State Court's decision to vacate the convictions of the five was not a declaration of innocence; rather it was a ruling that the new Reyes evidence would have affected their trials. In America, a person is innocent until proven guilty. Since the verdicts were vacated, those originally accused must be considered innocent. But still I ask myself, Were the five young men involved in my rape and beating? It is possible. Were the five wrongfully convicted? That is possible too. The young men served their prison time. I'd be heartsick if it is proved they were wrongfully sent to jail; society itself would be diminished. But almost without question, absolute proof does not exist, and I'll never know for sure. Acceptance of this uncertainty has eased the turmoil and the confusion, but they will never really go away.

Feelings about Reyes and the justice system overlie a deeper feeling I've experienced since the book was published: joy. It was hugely difficult to go public with the details of my love life, the fact of my anorexia, and the intimacies of my continuing disabilities. I'm an intensely private person, brought up to be ashamed of any deficiencies, and I sometimes wonder how strangers view me as a rape survivor with a brain injury. One positive result of the attack, however, is that it forced me to grow in ways I might not have otherwise. I no longer want to be the ultimate achiever, the "perfect" woman my mother brought me up to be. Instead, I've become more expert in being human, and that means flawed, vulnerable, tolerant of myself and others just as we are.

Yet I *did* speak, and the result has confirmed that telling my story was the right thing to do. It has been a release. Overcoming my uneasiness with exposure encouraged and gave permission for others to speak out as well. A woman wrote that she was raped more than thirty years ago and never told anyone because she felt so ashamed. After reading my book, she told a close friend about her anguish and "felt a 1,000 pound weight drop off my shoulders"—she felt permission to tell her story. Another woman, a head injury survivor, told me, "It was nice to relate to someone who had gone through brain injury. I sincerely thought I was going nuts, but you brought me back to reality." And many dealing with all kinds of struggles write to say that reading my stories showed them they are not alone in their feelings, in their fight. Stories heal. Finding your voice means finding yourself.

The joy comes in this confirmation that we are all connected. The invisible energy that links us to one another is delicate but as definite as the gravity that holds my feet to the earth. The connection was invaluable throughout my days at Gaylord and Salomon. I believe in it more strongly now, not only as a means of recovery, but as an essential of life. Many have expressed their sense of connection to me because I've been in their thoughts for many years.

As they feel connected to me, so I to them. I feel it even in my reaction to whoever raped and beat me—for connection to others does not discriminate. I am linked to the five originally accused of attacking me, whether guilty or not, and to Matias Reyes who is definitely guilty. Though I was his victim, he must have been a victim of psychological torment that I cannot imagine. This in no way justifies his actions, but it allows me to deal with the sickness of the crime he committed against me. And it has allowed me to turn back to something over which I have control: my life.

Resources

For rape, abuse, and incest survivors, a respected national group to contact for referrals is:

Rape, Abuse & Incest National Network
635-B Pennsylvania Ave., SE
Washington, D.C. 20003
1-800-656-HOPE
www.rainn.org

A respected national group for those with brain injuries:

Brain Injury Association of America
105 North Alfred Street
Alexandria, VA 22314
703-236-6000

1-800-444-6443 (Family Helpline)
www.biausa.org

For SAVI, contact:
Sexual Assault and Violence Intervention Program
The Mount Sinai Hospital of Mount Sinai NYU
    Health
Box 1670
One Gustave L. Levy Place
New York, NY 10029
212-423-2140 (Manhattan)
718-736-1288 (Queens)
www.mssm.edu/SAVI

For Gaylord, contact:
Gaylord Hospital
Gaylord Farm Road
P.O. Box 400
Wallingford, CT 06492
203-284-2800 or
1-866-GAYLORD
www.gaylord.org

For Achilles, contact:
The Achilles Track Club
Fourth Floor
42 West 38th Street
New York, NY 10018
212-354-0300
www.achillestrackclub.org

Further Reading

When we go through traumatic times we look for comfort and guidance from many sources, such as family, friends, spiritual beliefs, and books. A few books that helped are mentioned in the text. Here is a more complete list of books that were particularly useful during my recovery.

Chopra, Deepak, M.D. *Quantam Healing: Exploring the Frontiers of Mind/Body Medicine.*

Crimmins, Cathy. *Where Is the Mango Princess?*

Gordon, James S., M.D. *Manifesto for a New Medicine: Your Guide to Healing Partnerships and the Wise Use of Alternative Therapies.*

Hahn, Thich Nhat. *Peace Is Every Step: The Path of Mindfulness in Every Step.*

Hahn, Thich Nhat. *The Miracle of Mindfulness.*

Johnson, Spencer, M.D. *The Precious Present.*

Kabat-Zinn Jon, Ph.D. *Full-Catastrophe Living: Using the Wisdom of Your Body and Mind to Face Stress, Pain, and Illness.*

Kabat-Zinn, Jon, Ph.D. *Wherever You Go, There You Are: Mindfulness Meditation in Everyday Life.*

Moyers, Bill. *Healing and the Mind.*

Muller, Wayne. *Sabbath: Restoring the Sacred Rhythm of Rest.*

Sacks, Oliver, M.D. *A Leg to Stand On.*

Schwartz, Jeffery, M.D., and Sharon Begley. *The Mind and the Brain: Neuroplasticity and the Power of Mental Force.*

Siegel, Bernie S., M.D. *Love, Medicine, and Miracles: Lessons Learned about Self-Healing from a Surgeon's Experience with Exceptional Patients.*

The Institute of Noetic Sciences. *The Heart of Healing.*

Remen, Rachel Naomi, M.D. *Kitchen Table Wisdom: Stories That Heal.*

Remen, Rachel Naomi, M.D. *My Grandfather's Blessing: Stories of Strength, Refuge, and Belonging.*

Weil, Andrew, M.D. *Spontaneous Healing: How to Discover and Embrace Your Body's Natural Ability to Maintain and Heal Itself.*

Books mentioned in the text:

p. 117. Dossey, Larry, M.D. *Reinventing Medicine: Beyond Mind-Body to a New Era of Healing.*

p. 137. Herman, Judith Lewis, Ph.D. *Trauma & Recovery.*

p.119. Raine, Nancy Venable. *After Silence: Rape & My Journey Back.*

p.119. Sebold, Alice. *Lucky.*

Acknowledgments

My special thanks to Richard Marek, my collaborator in the writing, who captured my voice and helped me tell my story with the clarity I wanted.

Thanks also to Jim Davis for the contacts that helped start this project; to my agent, Joni Evans; to my adviser, Lisa Shotland; to my attorney, Larry Shire; to my "second reader," Dalma Heyn; to my editor at Scribner, Beth Wareham; and to all the others at Scribner whose support made publishing so easy and exciting and who treated me, my story, and my message with sensitivity and dignity.

And, for everything, from the bottom of my heart my thanks to Jim.